# BEEN THERE, DONE THAT

**GROSSET & DUNLAP**

An Imprint of Penguin Random House

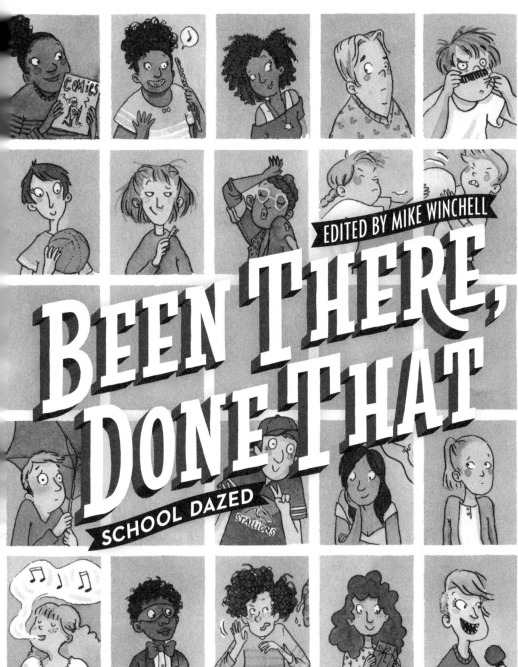

EDITED BY MIKE WINCHELL

# BEEN THERE, DONE THAT

SCHOOL DAZED

STALLIONS

FOR
ART STAFFORD,
WHO'S ALWAYS WATCHING
OVER US.

## GROSSET & DUNLAP

Penguin Young Readers Group
An Imprint of Penguin Random House LLC

Penguin supports copyright. Copyright fuels creativity, encourages
diverse voices, promotes free speech, and creates a vibrant culture.
Thank you for buying an authorized edition of this book and for complying
with copyright laws by not reproducing, scanning, or distributing any part
of it in any form without permission. You are supporting writers and
allowing Penguin to continue to publish books for every reader.

The publisher does not have any control over and does not assume
any responsibility for author or third-party websites or their content.

"Standing Tall" by Holly Goldberg Sloan is the basis for the
novel *Short*, which will be published in January 2017 by Dial Books
for Young Readers, an imprint of Penguin Random House.

Collection copyright © 2016 by Mike Winchell. Cover illustration
copyright © 2016 by Eglantine Ceulemans. All rights reserved.
Published by Grosset & Dunlap, an imprint of Penguin Random House LLC,
345 Hudson Street, New York, New York 10014. GROSSET & DUNLAP
is a trademark of Penguin Random House LLC. Printed in the USA.

*Library of Congress Cataloging-in-Publication Data is available.*

ISBN 9780448486741     10 9 8 7 6 5 4 3 2 1

# CONTENTS

# Dances and Talent Shows

# Bus Ride

# School's Out

# School Abroad

★ ★ ★

# Foreword

At the start of each new school year, you have lots of questions. What will this year be like? Will you make new friends? And the teachers—what do they have in store for you? How about projects and assignments, or special events like talent shows? There's so much to think about!

To help you navigate through your school daze, an awesome collection of authors has shared their own school experiences. Then they showed how they've used those experiences to write some pretty cool stories. Some might seem unbelievable. Some might be exactly what you're going through. And some ... well ... some might be downright weird.

Happy reading,
Mike Winchell
Editor

Mike Winchell

# Morning Routine

## The school day is about to begin.

Are you already in your seat with your notebook out, pencil in hand? Or is it a mad dash to your first class, sliding through the door as the bell rings? Either way, the morning announcements wait for no one, so listen up!

Shaun David Hutchinson knows all about the morning announcements, since he helped broadcast them daily in the television studio at his school. But in the story inspired by his experience, the announcements are a whole lot stranger.

# UNSEEN

ran toward the library, my shoelaces untied, the corner of my algebra book poking through my backpack and jabbing into my hip. I stubbed my shoe and stumbled. After looking down for a moment to catch my balance, I ran into and nearly through Max. He was standing in the open doorway, wearing his you're-so-freaking-late frown.

Max had embraced his inner nerd—his jutting front teeth and conspicuous oversize, inch-thick glasses made it difficult to hide—and I wasn't exactly popular, either, so we got along well.

I followed him into the library and turned right down the hallway that led to the TV studio. I popped into the control room first, hoping it was empty so I could take a moment to breathe, but Jimmy was lounging in one of the two chairs, his enormous sneakers propped on the edge of the desk. Mrs. Moody stood behind him, lecturing him about something he'd done. If Max was our resident tech geek, Jimmy was our troublemaker, sarcastic and hilariously rude. Only his winning smile saved him from perpetual detention.

Mrs. Moody was willowy, with a hair-sprayed helmet of brassy curls. The Warrior News Network was the only class she taught; she spent the rest of the day running the school library, which was a task better suited to her high-strung temperament. It didn't help that Jimmy took sadistic pleasure from winding her up and watching her shoot off in whichever direction he pointed her. But I wasn't in the mood to spend the morning dodging her anger, so I handed her a book she'd loaned me and asked for another, appealing to her librarian nature.

The gambit worked, and Mrs. Moody left us alone.

Jimmy thanked me. As much as he enjoyed tormenting her, he enjoyed peace and quiet more. His skin was tan from hours spent surfing before and after school, and his legs were yeti-hairy.

I asked Jimmy what he'd done to get Mrs. Moody so riled up. He rolled his eyes. "Told Molly she has a face for radio."

I grimaced and shoved Jimmy's legs off the desk so I could sit in the other chair. There were two control boards separated by three small monitors—one for each camera in the studio and one displaying our live broadcast. Max was the only person in our class who really understood what all the buttons and knobs did, and the only one Mrs. Moody trusted not to accidentally broadcast something that would get her fired.

Jimmy was a senior who'd signed up for the morning news class because he thought it would be an easy A. The only equipment he knew how to use were the cameras, and all he had to do was point them in the right direction. He still managed to botch it up at least once a week. Unlike Molly, who took the class more seriously than anyone had a right to. We delivered the morning announcements, not breaking news.

Mrs. Moody had been hinting to Molly that she needed to give someone else a chance behind the news desk, a suggestion Molly continued to ignore. Not that any of the rest of us were clamoring to take her place. Max loved working in the control room, Kara didn't care where Mrs. Moody stuck her so long as she could spend the first half of the morning catching up on her homework, and no one was stupid enough to suggest letting Jimmy sit in front of a camera during our daily live broadcasts.

And I hadn't seriously considered it, either. I definitely didn't want to be like Molly. She was always throwing herself in front of a camera or microphone, because she believed with her soul that she was destined to become the next Mariah Carey or Julia Roberts. Maybe both if she was lucky. Either she didn't know or didn't care that everyone laughed at her behind her back, including me, which made me feel like a jerk because I was too scared to pursue my passion for writing with the same blind enthusiasm. I never admitted it, but I sort of admired her.

Plus, people knew who she was, and I told Jimmy so.

He blew me off.

Jimmy and I weren't friends—I wasn't dumb enough to believe sharing a class together meant he would ever acknowledge my existence outside of the control room or studio—but he was easy to talk to, mostly because he never took anything seriously.

I asked him if he'd ever just wanted people to see him, to

know who he was. I asked him if he'd ever felt invisible. Which, of course, he hadn't, because he was good-looking and popular, and guys like him assumed that everyone was looking at them all the time.

People like Jimmy couldn't understand what it felt like for people to look through them as if they didn't exist. But I did. Sometimes I'd walk down the halls, on my way from one class to the next, and I'd want to stop and scream as loud as I could so all the students and teachers would see me. Really see me. So that they'd know who I was and that I existed.

When I explained some of what I was thinking to Jimmy, he told me that I thought too much. It wasn't an earth-shattering revelation, but he wasn't wrong, and I decided that I was going to tell Mrs. Moody I wanted to get in front of the cameras and read the announcements. I wanted people to remember me as more than the kid who nearly broke his nose when he ran into a cement column in the hallway, or the kid who slept in class so often that he had the impression of a spiral ring from a notebook permanently etched into his cheek.

I left the control room and wandered into the studio, where the lights were brighter and everything felt more real. Molly was going on and on about how boring the announcements were and how we should spice them up by adding a musical number. I tried to interrupt, but they didn't notice me.

Molly could have gone on for hours listing all the ways she could improve the program. Most of her suggestions likely would have served to showcase her varying talents, which seemed limitless in her own mind. Mrs. Moody finally and thankfully cut Molly off and told her to write down her ideas so she could evaluate them at a less hectic time.

"You know what would make the announcements better?" Max said from behind the camera, where he was on one knee messing with the cables. "Vampires. Robots, too, but I doubt we have the budget for them."

Classic Max. We were also on the debate team together. People teased him for looking weird and talking openly about his love of science fiction and computers, but he was actually a pretty cool guy. Mrs. Moody, however, didn't appreciate his humor. She turned to me and asked me what I wanted.

This was my chance. Her being annoyed with Molly could only improve the odds she'd agree to let me read the announcements. Even though the idea of sitting at the cheap desk and speaking at the camera while the whole school watched scared the pants off of me, I knew if I did it, people would see me. They would remember me instead of forgetting me the day after I graduated. But when I opened my mouth to ask, the words dried up. I shook my head and told her it was nothing.

Mrs. Moody nodded, clapped her hands, and told us to prepare for the broadcast. We were on in fifteen minutes.

I could always tell her tomorrow. Yeah. Maybe tomorrow, I thought.

The problem with tomorrow is that it's *always* tomorrow and never today.

# Shaun David Hutchinson

# PLEASE REMAIN CALM

clear my throat and look into the camera. Skye Bolton is sitting beside me, her bright green hair tied into a ponytail, her cheeks round and high, her perfect teeth filed to perfect points. Nelson stands behind the camera, holding three fingers out at his side. His wavy brown hair hangs over his eyes, and he watches me with a goofy grin.

Two . . .

One . . .

The red light begins to blink. Oh, how I loathe that red light. Life becomes more real the moment it begins to glow. Second chances evaporate when the camera is on, while I evaporate when it's off. I feel the eyes of every student at Sprawl High School turn toward me, watching, waiting for me to screw up. I can't actually see them, of course. The camera beams my face into a hundred classrooms on campus, but the process doesn't work in reverse. Still, I imagine them staring back at me. The only reason I do this is that, despite my anxiety, despite the fear that crawls like a hundred azagoth spiders up my legs and back

7

and arms, I know that this is the only time I'm truly seen.

Skye kicks me under the table.

"Good morning, students, teachers, and nonhuman friends. I'm Colt Favre, and this is your Sprawl Morning News. Please remain calm." My voice is froggy and thick. Ms. Briar hovers behind the glass in the control room and flashes me an exaggerated clown smile, miming with her wrinkled, blue-veined hands for me to do the same. I force my lips apart and raise my cheeks, but I feel like an orangutan baring its teeth.

"The singularity in the quantum physics lab has been contained. However, if you see Dr. Eisenhauer anywhere on campus, do *not* approach him under any circumstances. Especially if he's still glowing blue." I shuffle the papers on the desk in front of me. The pages are blank. Empty. Much like the minutes and hours and days of my life when I'm not in front of the camera.

"During the azagoth mating season, students are reminded that the tennis courts are off-limits. You know how hungry a breeding azagoth can be." I say the last sentence with a chuckle. "Seriously, though, eight students were cocooned and eaten during last year's mating season, and Principal Blake is hoping we can keep that number under five this year."

Nelson gives me a thumbs-up to let me know they've switched to the camera focused on Skye. The red light is still glowing, but I breathe a little easier.

"Now for sports," Skye says. She enunciates each syllable precisely. I once caught her in the girls' restroom drinking black tar from a stone bowl before repeating, "Theophilus

Thistler, the thistle sifter, in sifting a sieve of unsifted thistles, thrust three thousand thistles through the thick of his thumb," seven times. Ms. Briar would have given her detention for sure if she discovered Skye offering a sacrifice to the Dreadlies before a broadcast. Not that I would have snitched. I value my life, such as it is.

"Your Mighty Leviathans boys' basketball team massacred the Jupiter High Warriors after last night's devastating 98 to 22 loss. Better luck next time, boys!" Skye mugs for the camera like this is some worldwide broadcast rather than a lame high school news program that students only watch because their teachers chain them to their desks.

"The Lady Leviathans fared far better in their matchup against the Arkham Angels, bringing home a 65 to 48 win. However, Genevieve McMurtry lost a leg during the game, a crippling injury that will likely bench her for the remainder of the season. But don't worry, she's got three more, and the fourth should grow back in time for her to play next year."

Even with my anxiety in front of the camera, I become invisible when it's not focused on me. I disappear. If it weren't for the Sprawl Morning News, I don't think anyone at this school would even know I exist. They walk right past me in the halls, and teachers never call on me to answer questions, even when I raise my hand. I feel like I could fade away into nothing, and not one person would miss or even remember me.

Skye continues. "Tryouts for wrestling are being held Thursday in the gym. All suppliants are required to provide

Coach Shelley with parental and medical consent forms, your blood type, and two kittens. Preferably alive.

"And I'm happy to report that the cross-country track team placed third overall in last week's meet. Though parents were initially skeptical about Coach Villanova's plan to incorporate zombies into her training regimen, the surviving runners certainly proved them wrong." She glances at me. The spotlights reflect off her teeth, and I swear I can still see a little speck of tar on her canine. "Back to you, Colt."

Taking this class was a lark. My choices were the Sprawl News Network or Life Skills, and I wasn't keen on taking a class with a body count higher than Genghis Khan's. I didn't know how much I would grow to crave being in front of the camera. It was pure luck that Ms. Briar even allowed me to try out for the anchor position. Martina, who's in the control room with Ms. Briar, was the more logical choice. Her voice sometimes causes hallucinations and psychopathic tendencies, but only in boys who are especially susceptible. Before taking this class, my sole ambition was to survive until graduation, and I'd never given a single thought to what might happen after. Not that anyone could blame me. With a mortality rate hovering around 30 percent (still better than the district average), few students really think about the future until they're certain they'll live to see it.

And yet, as much as I despise that despotic, bloody light, I feel like I've found my calling. Unlike Skye, I don't crave glory or fame; I simply want to be seen.

I cough to cover the dead air, and continue. "The theater

department's performance of *A Delicious Murder* is being held this weekend in the Stoker Auditorium. Tickets are seven dollars in advance and ten dollars at the door. In this bold and inventive original murder mystery, audience members will help cast members solve a grisly homicide, and one lucky audience member will even have the opportunity to be the victim. All students must provide a parental consent form and next of kin when purchasing a ticket."

Skye croaks out a strangled laugh. "If it's anything like last year's production of *Little Shop of Horrors*, I'd advise attendees in the front row to bring a raincoat."

"You can say that again, Skye. I never did get the bloodstains out of my jeans."

I hate when she improvises. She only does it because she knows it throws me off, and everyone at school knows she has a compulsive need to be the center of attention. Last year, when Christye Bingham was crowned Homecoming Queen, Skye hid out behind the gym, raised a netherbeast, and set it loose in the gym. Then she tried to kill it on her own — she didn't even have a proper silver athame — so she could parade around as a hero and steal the spotlight from Christye. It didn't turn out quite the way Skye planned. Devin Moskowitz ended up taking down the netherbeast, and Skye lost a couple of toes. Unlike Genevieve's leg, Skye's toes won't regenerate.

I shuffle my blank papers while I try to remember the next announcement. Nelson holds up a cue card that says "Science fair," to remind me. I don't know what I'd do without that kid. It's really too bad his parents auctioned off his soul when he was a baby. But they did get a sweet car out of the deal, so I guess it evens out.

"When . . . um . . . if . . . don't forget to congratulate the winners of this year's science fair," I say, scrambling to regain my composure. Ms. Briar shakes her head, and I'm sure the mics pick up laughter from the control room. So unprofessional. "Runner-up Esteban Morales wowed judges by reanimating the corpse of Principal Blake, whose first act was to suspend Gregory Peters for killing him — crossbow safety is no laughing matter. But the real star of the science fair was Anya Mahadeo, whose demonstration of an interdimensional portal into the Bygone Lands earned her first prize. Mr. Kowalski is holding Anya's trophy for her in the event she manages to return with her sanity intact. We're rooting for you, Anya!"

Nelson visibly relaxes as the focus returns to Skye. He flashes me a goofy smile, which hopefully means I haven't botched up the show beyond all repair. Skye's been in Ms. Briar's ear for the last month to let her do the morning show alone, and if I keep screwing up, Ms. Briar might actually consider it. Without these few minutes a day to be seen, I wouldn't have any reason to bother showing up for school at all.

Skye tilts her head slightly to the side when she resumes speaking. "Vice Principal Brezenoff is asking anyone with information regarding the theft of twenty live frogs from the biology lab to report to him in the administration building.

"And for lunch today, the cafeteria is serving meat stew. Sounds yummy!"

To get back at Skye for interrupting me earlier, I turn and say, "Seems like our veep should investigate the meat stew if he really wants to find those frogs."

But Skye hardly misses a beat. "Don't be silly, Colt, you know they'd never serve us something as extravagant as frog. But those azagoths on the tennis court better watch out. Chef Lafferty is a whiz with a cleaver." She laughs so hard, she nearly snorts, yet still manages to make it look rehearsed and professional, before moving right into the next announcement.

"For all you juniors and seniors watching, prom has been moved from May twenty-first to May fourteenth to avoid coinciding with the full moon. Your offering to Carthaxis will be accepted at the door, and students are reminded that only bladed, noncursed weapons are allowed inside the hall."

I can't bear to think about prom. Shane Augustino didn't even acknowledge me when I asked him. Shane Augustino, of all people! If I can't get a guy with that much body hair and a tail to be my date, I'm going to wind up sitting at home watching my parents perform ritual sacrifices all night. Dad says the problem is that I'm too normal. Everyone else is either the spawn of a Dreadly or the blood slave of one of the many faces of the Infinite Horde. How can I compete with that? I'm barely important enough for anyone to try to dismember and eat.

Skye, of course, is attending with Jeremy Weston. He's practically Sprawl royalty. His father is mayor, his mother the high priestess of Belarax. And he was born in a nightmare. A freaking nightmare! I wish I'd been born in a nightmare instead of in the back of a Ford Focus on the way to the hospital. If I had, maybe then I'd have gotten some cool supernatural powers. Once, I thought I could set things on fire because I burned down the chemistry lab, but it turned out someone had just forgotten to shut off the gas on a Bunsen burner.

The other day I thought about asking someone to prom during a broadcast. Then everyone in the school would hear me, they'd see me. And he'd have to say yes. Only I didn't know who to ask. The truth is that I'm just not good enough for anyone. I can't think of a single person who wouldn't drown themselves to avoid going to prom with me. Besides, if I pulled a stunt like that, Ms. Briar would yank me out from in front of the cameras for sure, and I'd spend the rest of the year completely invisible.

Nelson is waving at me again, and I realize that I'm up. I smile at Nelson for saving my skin, and he winks back.

"The debate team has asked us to remind you that you are wrong. The *Leviathan Weekly* regrets to announce that, due to the extra space necessary for obituaries, they will no longer be printing the popular haruspicy advice column "Questions of the Heart and Other Internal Organs." And the mathletes are on the hunt for new members. If you love confluent hypergeometric functions and you've got the brains, see Mrs. Spalding to sign up. If you don't have the brains, they have extras to loan you."

"Maybe I should check that out," Skye says. "What do you think, Colt?"

This time I'm ready and refuse to let her fluster me. "Oh, Skye, I doubt they'll let you eat those brains, but I know that

14

won't stop you from trying." She kicks me under the desk again, and this time it's Nelson who can't stop laughing. Ms. Briar is flapping her arms like she's going to smash through the glass separating the studio from the control booth and strangle us.

"Finally," I say, "we'd like to take a moment to remember those students and faculty we've lost this week. With any luck, they'll turn up alive."

"I wouldn't count on it," Skye says with a bitter laugh.

"That's it for us here at Sprawl Morning News. I'm Colt Favre—"

"And I'm Skye Bolton."

"—have a wonderful day, and we hope you'll survive to tune in tomorrow. All hail Mighty Belarax."

I count to three and watch the red lights on both cameras die.

"You are such a loser!" Skye screeches at me the moment we're off the air. "I hate you!" She stands up, sending her chair skittering back into the wall behind her, and storms out of the studio.

It's a small victory, but I cherish it, anyway. She's got everything I want. Popularity, a boyfriend, people who see and pay attention to her when she talks. She doesn't know how fortunate she is.

I stand slowly. Without the cameras on me, I'm already fading, disappearing.

"Great show, Colt," Nelson says. He's all smiles.

"Yeah. Whatever."

My hands are translucent; I can see the speckled linoleum floor through my legs.

"That last bit with Skye was killer." Nelson edges out from behind the camera. "She's so mad."

"I guess."

The overhead studio lights beam through my body like it's made of glass.

"So, I've been meaning to ask you something," Nelson says. As my body loses cohesion, his words pass through me.

"Sure," I say, not really hearing him.

"Cool. I was wondering if . . ."

I hold my hands in front of my face and watch them vanish. Until nothing remains. In moments I transform from the face of Sprawl High News, seen by hundreds, to an afterimage that fades and is soon forgotten. Like always. I drift to the door like a dandelion seed carried by an easterly breeze. I don't say good-bye to Ms. Briar or Nelson or anyone. They wouldn't hear me if I tried.

"And it'd be such a blast. We could rent a limo and wear matching tuxes and . . ." Nelson's voice trails after me, but the words are little more than a meaningless jumble of sounds. They don't register. I barely perceive them before I float out of the studio. He's still talking and he can't even see me. I'm not even there. What was he asking me? I'm sure it wasn't important.

Sometimes I don't know why I bother with school at all.

But that's a lie. I do know.

I want to be seen.

Mike Winchell

# CLASS HAS STARTED

**Congratulations, you've made it to** your first class! There's your teacher, the person who will introduce you to all kinds of new things, from study skills, to important information, to lasting life lessons.

The thing is—as you will learn from authors Howard Cruse, Meg Medina, and Bruce Coville—every teacher has a unique style. Some can be a bit strange with an odd sense of humor, some are stern and direct, while others are sensitive, encouraging, and want to connect with students on multiple levels. But one thing they have in common is that they all have helpful lessons to share.

# DARING TO BE DOC

Doc, our Basic Studies teacher, was normally punctual, but on one memorable occasion he threatened to be a no-show for class. And an unwritten rule at my boarding school was that should a teacher fail to arrive, his students were duty bound to wait patiently for ten minutes but no longer. After that grace period, they were free to return to their dorm rooms.

Those ten minutes of waiting time were usually boring. Which is why, that day during my freshman year when the starting bell rang and Doc was nowhere to be seen, I impulsively chose to fill the dead time with improvised entertainment for the benefit of my captive classmates.

*Basic Studies*, I should explain, was the umbrella term for a class that from day to day rotated its emphasis among writing, history, literature, and philosophy. The inclusion of philosophy among the more typical ninth-grade disciplines was due to Doc's presence among the course's rotating set of teachers. Philosophical inquiries were among Doc's favorite pastimes, and he especially enjoyed engaging in them with the school's teenage population. He saw that as a good way to open young minds to new ways of looking at life.

Doc and I had bonded from my earliest days at the school. He found my cartooning ambitions a refreshing novelty, and he encouraged me to let my satirical impulses roam free. This was true even when he was my target, as he often was in the cartoons I drew for the student newspaper.

Spoofing Doc was easy because of the unique figure he cut as an educator. He was a tall, portly, big-boned, balding, pipe-puffing, charismatic visionary whose brilliance was obvious even though he spoke in a rural Oklahoma drawl.

In or out of the classroom, Doc was likely to prod students into conversations about topics we had never seriously considered, like the nature of democracy or the essentials of civic responsibility. For a teenager like me he was an inspiring presence. His role as a mentor didn't stop me from making fun of him, though.

On the mornings when Doc took the Basic Studies helm, he always began by puffing on his pipe as he spelled out on the blackboard the area of philosophical inquiry he had chosen for the day. A typical example might be:

*Proposition: A chair does not exist if I cannot see it.*

Lively arguments and counterarguments would soon be sparked among Doc and the kids in the room.

Which brings me to the day Doc showed up late for class. Most of my classmates were happy to swap jokes and otherwise goof off during our unexpected ten minutes of leisure, but I surprised myself by leaping to my feet and strolling to the blackboard, where I scrawled some absurd philosophical proposition that I've long since forgotten and began improvising a comic impression of Doc's style of teaching.

My startled classmates locked their eyes on me and began chuckling. No one was rolling in the aisles, but the laughs I got kept me riffing.

So I spent several minutes satirizing all of Doc's mannerisms I could think of. His drawl was the centerpiece, of course, but puffing on an imaginary pipe filled out the picture, as did furrowing my brow while I waited for my classmates to answer questions that—unlike any questions Doc might really ask—everyone knew were ridiculous.

But my stomach quaked when I noticed the face of our late-arriving teacher peering through the window of our classroom door. I had no need to worry, though, because Doc, quickly perceiving what was going on, chose not to interrupt my improvisation. I was being creative, after all, which he enjoyed when I did it on paper and which still tickled him now that I was doing it in the flesh. The good-natured sparkle I saw in his eyes gave me courage to carry on.

So I did.

For a bit too long.

Giddy from the laughter I had initially elicited from my peers, I began realizing that my improvisatory skills were running out of steam. My humor was wearing thinner, my audience becoming less amused. But I was unable to invent a good way to bring my stunt to a close.

Finally one of my classmates solved the problem for me. He stood up, grumbled, "This is a big waste of time," and headed for the door. Before his hand could touch the doorknob, though, Doc stepped into the room, and the student retreated.

For a moment I froze. Then I reassumed the role of compliant student by sheepishly surrendering the floor to Doc. Without commenting on what had just transpired, Doc wrote the day's philosophical proposition on the board, and the format of our normal Basic Studies class was restored.

After class, I found Doc strolling alongside me down the hall. He drawled, "Well, Howard, that was fun, but a good performer knows when it's time to get off the stage."

I KNEW FROM AN EARLY AGE THAT I WAS A **DORK**.

IT WAS A **GIVEN!**

DORK! DORK! DORK! DORK! DORK! DORK!

I KNEW THE SCORE EVEN BEFORE ALL THE **OTHER** KIDS AT SCHOOL STARTED **INFORMING** ME OF THE FACT.

STILL, I THOUGHT I JUST **MIGHT** HAVE A **CHANCE** IN LIFE IF I COULD LEARN TO BE A...

# FUNNY DORK!

BUT WHAT MAKES A GUY **FUNNY**? I NEEDED A BOOK THAT WOULD **TELL** ME.

THIS OUGHTA DO IT!

HOW TO BE A COMEDIAN

AND IT'S GOT A WHOLE SECTION OF **FAMOUS JOKES** IN THE BACK.

**HERE'S** ONE THAT'S PRETTY FUNNY.

I'LL TRY IT OUT ON MY **BROTHER**.

HEY, BILLY, "MY WIFE IS SO **UGLY** THAT WHEN SHE LOOKS IN A **MIRROR**, IT'S **HER FACE** THAT CRACKS."

YOU **DORK!** THAT'S THE **STUPIDEST** THING YOU'VE EVER **SAID!**

LIKE **YOU'RE** EVER GONNA HAVE A **WIFE!**

YOU DON'T EVEN KNOW HOW TO GET A **DATE!**

**U**NRECEPTIVE AUDIENCES! A NIGHTMARE FOR US **COMEDIANS**.

MY BEST FRIEND (AND FELLOW DORK), **LYDIA**, HAD USEFUL **ADVICE** FOR ME.

WHY DON'T YOU WATCH SOME **OTHER** PEOPLE BEING FUNNY AND SEE HOW **THEY** DO IT?

NOT A BAD **IDEA**...

©2015 by H. Cruse

I BEGAN DEVOTING ALL MY FREE TIME TO **RESEARCH**.

LET'S SEE...WHO DO I KNOW AROUND THE SCHOOL WHO'S **FUNNY**?

MY CLASSMATE **SPUD** WAS DEFINITELY SOMETHING OF A **CUT-UP**.

HAW! HAW!

OW!

HAW! HAW!

BOINK!

BUT HE WASN'T **REMOTELY** DORKY ENOUGH TO SERVE AS A **ROLE MODEL** FOR ME.

**BERNICE** WAS GREAT AT GETTING **LAUGHS**, BUT **SHE WAS POPULAR**!

YUK, YUK!

I CAN'T BELIEVE YOU **SAID** THAT, BERNICE!

I **KNEW** I DIDN'T HAVE A CHANCE OF PULLING **THAT** OFF.

**MARLENE** HAD A REAL **TALENT** FOR **DRY WIT**.

Chuckle!

OF COURSE, JUST BEING **WITTY** HAS ALWAYS BEEN **BEYOND** ME...

...MUCH LESS BEING **DRY** AT THE SAME **TIME**.

HEY, AREN'T WE SUPPOSED TO BE HEADING FOR **ENGLISH** AROUND NOW?

LEAVE DISHES HERE

OOPS! I LOST TRACK OF **TIME**!

Y'KNOW, YOU SHOULD KEEP AN EYE ON **MR. TUTTLE**. HE'S PRETTY FUNNY AS **TEACHERS** GO.

MR. TUTTLE, OUR ENGLISH TEACHER, WAS KNOWN AS A SCHOOL **"CHARACTER"** DUE TO HIS PENCHANT FOR **JOKING AROUND** ALL THE TIME IN HIS CLASSES.

HMM.

♪

AHEM!!

FOR EXAMPLE, HE ALWAYS MADE A BIG **PRODUCTION** OUT OF SIMPLY WALKING INTO HIS **CLASSROOM** EVERY DAY.

HE **TWISTED** HIS **MUSTACHE** LIKE A **MELODRAMA VILLAIN** EVERY TIME HE GAVE OUT **HOMEWORK**.

YOU'LL JUST **LOVE** WHAT I'VE GOT IN STORE FOR YOU **THIS** TIME! cackle!

IT WAS ALMOST **SADISTIC,** THE WAY HE'D **HUMILIATE** ANY POOR KID WHO GOT AN **ANSWER WRONG...**

*Sob!* HAVE **MERCY** ON ME, JESS!

HA! HA! HA!

YOU'RE GOING TO **PULVERIZE** MY **PEDAGOGICAL REPUTATION!**

...BUT HE'D HAVE EVERY-ONE **ELSE** IN THE ROOM IN **STITCHES** WHEN HE **DID** IT.

EVEN IF YOU GOT AN ANSWER **RIGHT,** YOU WEREN'T NECESSARILY **HOME FREE.**

HA! HA! HA!

YOU KIND OF, UH, ♪ **WHOOPSY-DOOPSY STUMBLED** ♪ ONTO THAT ANSWER, **DIDN'T** YOU, BEA?

AND **WOE** BE TO ANY STUDENT WHO DARED TO LOOK LIKE HE WAS **DROWSY** IN CLASS.

SHALL I GIVE YOU SOME **SNORING LESSONS,** OWEN?

HA HA HA

HA!

---

I SCRIBBLED **NOTES** AS **INCONSPICUOUSLY** AS I COULD, TRYING TO HOLD ON TO EACH AND EVERY **ODDITY** IN MR. TUTTLE'S **BEHAVIOR.**

Let's see now...Diddly diddly doodly ♪ doo...

IT WAS ALL I COULD **THINK** ABOUT AT **HOME.**

♪ Diddly doodly diddly doo...

GORDON, TWIRLING YOUR **FORK** ISN'T GOING TO GET ANY **PEAS** INTO YOUR MOUTH.

*Snicker!* WOTTA **DORK!**

IN MY HEAD AT NIGHT, I PRACTICED MR. TUTTLE'S QUIRKY **HABITS**—LIKE **PACING** BACK AND FORTH AND **PINCHING** HIS **LIP** WHILE HE TALKED.

I FELT **FUNNIER** BY THE DAY.

Heh heh!

---

I HAD NO WAY OF KNOWING THAT ALL OF THIS **THINKING** WAS GOING TO HAVE AN UNEXPECTED **PAYOFF...**

HEY, WHERE'S **MR. TUTTLE?**

...ON A DAY WHEN MR. TUTTLE HAPPENED TO BE UNCHARACTERISTICALLY **LATE** TO OUR **CLASS.**

HE'S NOT **COMING?**

THE **BELL** RANG **TEN** MINUTES AGO.

D'YA THINK HE'S GONNA BE A **NO-SHOW...?**

AS THE ROOM BUZZED WITH **CONFUSION,** I WAS GRIPPED BY A STRANGE, **GIDDY** SENSATION.

YOU'RE GETTING A VERY WEIRD **LOOK** IN YOUR EYE, GORDON...

I COULD TELL I HAD MR. TUTTLE'S **PACING** AND **LIP-PINCHING** DOWN **COLD** FROM THE **GUFFAWS** OF **RECOGNITION**.

AND I WAS **DEFINITELY** NAILING THE FRETFUL **SQUEAK** THAT ALWAYS CREPT INTO HIS **VOICE** WHENEVER HE WAS CONFRONTED WITH A **DANGLING PARTICIPLE!**

I WAS ON **FIRE** WITH AN ALMOST **SCARY** RUSH OF **POWER**.

I WAS A **MASTER PUPPETEER**, GENERATING FRESH WAVES OF **LAUGHTER** WITH EVERY **SWOOP** OF MY **HAND**.

HA! HAW! HA! GUFFAW! HAW!

IT WAS A **MIRACLE!** ALL OF A SUDDEN I — **GORDON** THE **DORK** — WAS ACTUALLY BECOMING **POPULAR!**

OF COURSE, WHAT I HADN'T **PLANNED** FOR WAS THAT I WOULD EVENTUALLY RUN OUT OF FRESH **TUTTLE-ISMS** TO **SATIRIZE**.

UH-OH...

I TOOK TO **REPEATING** MYSELF, BUT NOTHING WAS AS **FUNNY** THE SECOND TIME AROUND.

THE **ENERGY** IN THE ROOM BEGAN **SAGGING**. THE **LAUGHS** BECAME LESS **FREQUENT**.

I SPOTTED A FEW KIDS **TEXTING** THEIR **FRIENDS** OR **YAWNING**. **THAT** DIDN'T BODE WELL...

click click click! click click!

**UNEASY GLANCES** WERE BEING EXCHANGED INSTEAD OF **GUFFAWS**.

I JACKED UP MY LEVEL OF **EXAGGERATION** IN A PATHETIC EFFORT TO REGAIN **GROUND**. **NOTHING HELPED**.

THAT'S WHEN I **REALIZED** FOR THE FIRST TIME THAT MR. TUTTLE HAD QUIETLY ENTERED THE CLASSROOM WHILE I WAS **MIMICKING** HIM.

PSST!

HE WAS STANDING JUST INSIDE THE DOOR, WATCHING MY EVERY **MOVE**.

HE HADN'T EVEN SAID **"AHEM!"** THAT WASN'T **FAIR!**

I HOPED AGAINST **HOPE** THAT HE WAS FINDING MY IMPERSONATION AT LEAST **MILDLY** ENTERTAINING... BUT **NO!**

I WAS LEARNING A REGRETTABLE **FACT** OF **LIFE:**

**P**EOPLE WHO ENJOY MAKING FUN OF **OTHER PEOPLE** DON'T ALWAYS ENJOY HAVING **OTHERS** MAKE FUN OF **THEM.**

**W**ITH THE PRESSURE ON, I WAS RUNNING OUT OF FUNNY STUFF TO **ADD.**

IT WAS OBVIOUSLY **PAST** TIME TO BRING THINGS TO A **CLOSE,** BUT I COULDN'T THINK HOW TO **DO** IT.

**I**N DESPERATION, I RESORTED TO ONE LAST **PLOY...**

UHH... MY WIFE IS SO **UGLY** THAT WHEN SHE LOOKS IN A **MIRROR,** IT'S **HER FACE** THAT CRACKS.

**N**OT A **TITTER.**

**O**NLY **SILENCE.**

? HUH? ?

HIS **WIFE??!**

**F**INALLY, ONE OF MY CLASSMATES STOOD UP AND **WHINED....**

MR. TUTTLE, COULD WE **PLEASE** GET ON WITH THE **CLASS?**

THIS IS A STUPID WASTE OF **TIME!**

**T**HAT CERTAINLY LET ANY REMAINING **AIR** OUT OF MY TIRES!

IT'S PRETTY **SAD** WHEN A DUMB **13-YEAR-OLD** WOULD RATHER GET HIS **ENGLISH CLASS** UNDERWAY THAN SPEND ONE MORE **MINUTE** BEING ENTERTAINED BY **YOU!**

# Meg Medina

# ALL THAT MRS. ZUCKERMAN TAUGHT ME

Every school has a Mrs. Zuckerman.

She's the teacher whom everyone dreams of having because there's light in her eyes and a sense of fun.

Mrs. Zuckerman taught the Talented and Gifted class, the smartest third-grade class at P.S. 22, where I went to elementary school. Everyone knew that was the class for minigeniuses, which made me feel a little hopeless at the end of second grade. I still used my fingers to do addition. Mrs. Kreitman, my teacher, had repeatedly pointed out my sloppy work habits in the comments section of my report card every quarter, too. I ate holes in my papers with my erasures, and my worksheets were always stained and crumpled. And, of course, there was my lingering fascination with Elmer's glue. I'd make little blobs inside my desk and play with them as they dried into gooey lumps.

What hope, then, did I have to be moved into Mrs. Zuckerman's group? Only the very best students were destined for that class, and I suspected that they had better work habits than mine. They remembered their homework and brought in elaborate projects. They certainly knew their number facts. My best skill was getting lost in a book or making up stories. Mrs. Kreitman had sometimes even called it daydreaming or lying.

Imagine my shock, then, when I peeked at my final report card and found Mrs. Zuckerman's name and room number. Was this a mistake? A joke? Even my mother was speechless over the miracle, but she didn't argue.

Naturally, I fell in love with Mrs. Zuckerman the way everyone always did. She was cheerful when we arrived each morning, and almost never raised her voice when we got too rambunctious. Instead, she quieted us with her own contagious stillness. She always assigned us interesting projects, too, especially in writing, my favorite. It was Mrs. Zuckerman, in fact, who wrote the words "Margaret, you are a wonderful writer" across the top of my first poem. It was the first time I could remember that a teacher said I was good at anything. I beamed inside and rewrote my final copy with more care than I had ever written anything else before. All these years later, when I look back to what made me love writing, I think it was Mrs. Zuckerman's approval and praise.

But Mrs. Zuckerman also taught me something even more important than having faith in my writing, and it happened on the heels of what I was sure was a disaster.

As the winter holiday break approached that year, all of the students buzzed about the wonderful things they would bring Mrs. Zuckerman as a present. I already had the perfect plan.

Someone as spectacular as Mrs. Zuckerman deserved a truly spectacular gift. My choice was obvious. I would buy her a Chia Pet. To me, that pottery gift seemed magical. It was shaped like a sheep; you would water it, and within days the seeds inside would sprout to look like lamb's wool. Pointless? Maybe. But this was the era of mood rings and pet rocks, too.

Unfortunately, my mother had other ideas. In fairness, I have to admit that money was very limited in our family. My mother earned minimum wage, there were three mouths to feed, and the rent would soon be due. But the bigger problem was my mother's eccentricity, which made a scary companion to her tightwad tendencies. She was criminally practical, too. Every purchase she made had to be useful. In other words, she could be counted on to give you pencils and underwear as Christmas gifts.

Anyway, she hated my idea.

A hunk of pottery that grew grass seedlings to imitate fur? Who on earth would want such a thing, she said. Instead, Mami handed me the gift that she had carefully selected.

It was a pair of pantyhose that she had purchased at the supermarket for a dollar.

I begged my mother to see it my way, but it was no use. I was destined to die of shame. While my friends would shower Mrs. Zuckerman with impressive gifts, I would hand over a woman's personal undergarments. The only worse gift might have been a bra.

I walked to school that day, heavyhearted, and handed over the gift at the very last moment. Somehow that odd gift made me feel like an especially poor kid and, worse, a weird one. I was positive that no American family would ever stoop to give pantyhose as a present.

Thankfully, Mrs. Zuckerman chose not to open any of the gifts that day. When she hugged us each good-bye, she promised to do so over vacation.

When I got back to school in January, there were small white envelopes on our desks. My name was written in her beautiful script on the outside.

*Dear Margaret,*

*Thank you so much for the lovely and practical gift. I will get plenty of use from the hosiery. You were so thoughtful to think of me.*

*Your friend,*
*Mrs. Zuckerman*

There are so many ways that adults can build up children. We can teach them and put stars on their papers. We can laugh at their jokes. We can help them when they struggle with friends. Mrs. Zuckerman did all of those things, of course. But with that simple acknowledgment of my strange gift, she did something else. She erased all of my shame and gave me a living example of the power of extending even the simplest kindness.

# Meg Medina

# A PRESENT FOR MRS. ROBERTSON

Charlene Venuti has a lazy eye that makes her lean over her papers at school, but that has never once stopped her from noticing everything about everybody, all the time. Like now.

"What are *you* getting Mrs. Robertson?" Charlene asks me. "You have to tell." Emily and Kyoko look up from the cards they are drawing and wait.

Friday is the last day before vacation, and everyone will come to school with a present for our favorite fifth-grade teacher. The girls at Table Four have already gone shopping with their moms. Charlene bought earrings made of "almost real pearls," she says. Emily went to the ceramics studio on Long Island with her sister and painted a mug that they're going to fill with candies. Kyoko had her uncle bring back a pretty doll with a satin kimono from his business trip to Japan.

I reach for a scented marker and draw a blue snowflake. "It's a surprise," I say, taking in a whiff of fake blueberry. "But it's going to be perfect."

33

Charlene and Emily give each other a look that makes my stomach squeeze. *You're lying*, their eyes say as they go back to drawing their cards. I know that look. It's almost the same one they gave me when I was first assigned to Mrs. Robertson's class in September. *What are you doing here?* their eyes seemed to ask.

I'll admit it: Even I was shocked to see that I'd be spending fifth grade in the top class. I'm not a genius like Charlene and the other kids in here, like Kyoko, who plays the violin, or Sanjay, who does pre-algebra at the middle school every day at eleven. It's kind of a miracle, actually. Mrs. Mueller, my fourth-grade teacher, was always pointing out my sloppy desk with the papers sticking out, the holes I'd erased into my worksheets, the careless misspellings. "Slow down, Maria Elisa. Your mind is speeding too fast. Work carefully to let your ideas shine through!"

That's hard for me though, especially when I'm writing. Sometimes the ideas come to me so fast that my fingers just can't catch up to writing them. Maybe that was why they gave me to Mrs. Robertson. She is always telling us about new books to read. Still, I can't be sure, and Charlene has a different idea, of course.

"Mrs. Mueller is really old. She's going to retire in June," Charlene told me as part of her Table Four welcome wagon. "Maybe she's getting, you know, cuckoo, and made a mistake sending you here."

What I really want to know is who appointed Charlene chief

of the Brain Police in this class? She acts like it's her mission to sniff out the less-than-gifted. You can't get a paper back without her wanting to know your grade, her High Holy Days being report card time.

"How many Excellents did *you* get?" she asked a few weeks ago when we got our first-quarter grades. I ignored her. I'd gotten mostly Gs, for *good*, and an Excellent in Language Arts.

Naturally, Charlene had a long row of Es in everything from spelling to work habits, and she's always bragging. Her record, she informed me, is fourteen, "but who's counting?"

*You are*, I wanted to shout up her nose. *That's who!*

If I were Mrs. Robertson, I'd give Charlene a big fat U (for unbelievably annoying) in social skills.

Anyway, I'm not telling her what I have planned for Mrs. Robertson. Today is finally payday for my mom, and I'll go shopping after school to get it. I've had my eye on this present for weeks, and I know Mrs. Robinson will always think of me when she takes care of it.

Just then, the overhead lights flash. It's our class signal to stop what we're doing and look up. The clock reads two thirty-five.

"Cleanup time," Mrs. Robertson announces, with her hand on the light switch. "Another afternoon has flown!"

I pack up my things and stack my chair on my desk. Then we line up, sweating in our coats as we wait for Mrs. Robertson to say good-bye. She takes her time with dismissal, but somehow it's still my favorite time. She doesn't sprint for her car the way some people do. (Yes, I saw you, Mrs. Mueller.) Instead, she says good-bye to each of us separately as we file past her in line. If you've had a bad day, she says, "Tomorrow will be better," and doesn't look grouchy. If you've done well on a test, she gives you a high five. She'll tie a small piece of yarn around your finger to remind you to bring a form back. Sometimes, she just says simple things, like "It was fun having you in my class today." No other teacher at Thomas Jefferson Elementary does that.

The beads of sweat are running down my back by the time she finally gets to me. I'm the tallest girl, so I'm always last. I hate this puffy coat. It's my old one from last year. The dirt stains won't come out, and my wrists peek through.

When it's my turn, Mrs. Robertson puts her hands on my overly padded shoulders. "That was a wonderful poem you wrote today, Maria Elisa. I'm still thinking about it!"

My whole inside goes even warmer. Mrs. Robertson is teaching us how to write poems, and we can write about anything that matters to us. Today I wrote about trash, which some people at Table Four said was a dumb topic. I don't care. Newspapers, plastic straws, and used coffee cups blow into our playground all the time, and I hate it.

*Pollution is nasty; garbage is, too. Why isn't the sky a clear, clean blue?*

She read the whole thing out loud to the class.

"You're a poet and an environmental activist," she says as she flips off the lights and pulls the door closed.

"Thank you, Mrs. Robertson," I say.

And just like that, I forget all about how Charlene makes me feel.

★ ★ ★

I take the long way home along Ellwood Avenue and stop to look in the store windows as I go. I want to make sure they haven't sold out of what I want to buy for Mrs. Robertson. The air outside is chilly enough to cut through my coat, and there's a metallic scent in the air that tells me snow is on the way. My breath makes little clouds on the glass as I look at all the things I'd like to buy myself if I could. New hairbands and rainbow-colored toe socks. A new hoodie. A three-tier art set that folds out like stairs with markers, watercolors, and color pastels.

I won't get any of that, though. Mami already warned me that we're going to have a "simple *Navidad*" this year. That means one present for each of us. I hope she'll pick the art set and not another pair of "sturdy jeans at a good price" like last year. They looked like farmer pants, and they were so stiff that I couldn't even bend my knees in gym class for a month.

The real problem is that Mami never "wastes money," and almost everything qualifies as "waste." She cuts my hair (which explains my crooked bangs), and we never eat out anywhere, not even french fries at Bustlin' Burgers, which has the best ones. Mami would be much happier getting a toaster than any fancy perfume.

But Mrs. Robertson isn't like Mami. She wears lipstick, and she loves imagination. Plus, she's so supersmart and nice that she deserves something clever. Sure, she'll like her mug and her almost-real earrings and her satin-dressed doll. But I've chosen something that is even better.

And there it is, still sitting there in the middle of the storefront window at Gone Bananas Shop.

A Chia Pet.

★ ★ ★

Mami stares at me as I explain my idea.

I point to the picture in the flyer: a clay sheep covered in grassy hair.

"You put the chia seeds inside and water it, and it grows the fur," I tell her. "Isn't it fantastic? We learned about germination last month."

She's just gotten home from the Queen for a Day Laundromat, where she works as an attendant. Some people come with Santa Claus–size bags of dirty clothes, but she doesn't mind. Mami is the only person I know who actually loves doing laundry. "You can see the results of your effort," Mami says. Plus, not speaking English isn't a problem. All you need to say are the days of the week, numbers, and *Have a good day.*

She studies the flyer, scanning the words she doesn't understand. There's lint caught in the hinges of her glasses, and she smells pleasantly of detergent. Suddenly she frowns.

"*¡Diez dólares!*" Her eyes go wide. Ten dollars! "We can't go around buying people presents that cost ten dollars!"

"It's not just anybody, Mami. It's Mrs. Robertson!" I say. "She's my favorite *maestra*!"

"Do the math, Maria Elisa — and don't use your fingers! If we buy even five people something like that, we'll be out our grocery money for a whole week. We can't go hungry!"

*"Pero, Mami!"* I say, stumbling over my Spanish. My stomach is in a knot, and tears start to cloud my eyes. "A Chia Pet is perfect!"

"Don't be ridiculous!" Mami says. She slips off her shoes and stretches her back. "Why would she want that grassy thing? She's not a cow, for heaven's sake! *¡Que locura!*"

"It is *not* crazy!" I follow her to the kitchen, where she reaches under the sink for pots and pans to start dinner. "Mrs. Robertson loves science! Besides, everyone will give her a good present. It will be rude not to give her something. I'll be the only one who is empty-handed!"

She puts the pan on the burner, exasperated, and turns to me. "Who said you'd be empty-handed?"

I stop in my tracks, worried.

"I've already bought Mrs. Robertson a present," she continues. She opens the hall closet and pulls out a big plastic bag. "Your teacher is a working woman, like me." She fishes deep inside. "I know just . . . what . . . she needs."

She finally pulls out what she's looking for and holds it out to me.

I blink, hoping it's a mirage.

But no. It's real.

Mami is holding a packaged pair of pantyhose. The woman on the front is sitting half nude, her arms crossed across her naked breasts. The price in the corner says $1.49.

The room begins to spin. I imagine Mrs. Robertson opening this present in front of the class. I can already hear Charlene's laugh and the boys all ribbing one another and using words like *boobies.*

"No!" I cry.

"No?" Mami frowns. "What do you mean?"

"I can't give her that! It's all wrong!" Desperate, my tears start to flow. "That lady is naked, can't you see?"

"Don't overreact. She's covering herself modestly."

My voice is loud, and my nose is running. "Mami," I shout. "This is the dumbest gift ever!"

Mami's eyes become steely and dark. She doesn't like me to be fresh, and I can see that she's holding her back straight the way she always does when she's made a final decision.

"This is what we'll be giving her, *niña.*" She hands over a tube of Christmas paper. "Now, wrap it."

★ ★ ★

"So, where's your present?" Charlene asks me on Friday afternoon. We're having our holiday party, but I'm not in the mood. "Don't you have anything?" She narrows her eyes, waiting.

"It's there, Charlene." I give her an ugly look and bite the head off a candy cane reindeer.

I'm not lying, not technically. Mrs. Robertson's desk is covered with carefully wrapped presents, but mine is actually on the floor beneath her desk near the trash can, where it belongs. I sneaked back to our classroom during lunch and lodged it there, hoping that she won't see it.

"You're not fond of cupcakes, Maria Elisa?" Mrs. Robertson asks me. She's walking around the room with a tray of delicious-looking cupcakes frosted in red and green.

"No thanks," I say glumly. "I'm not very hungry."

Charlene grabs the biggest one. "When are you going to open your presents, Mrs. Robertson?" she asks, pointing at the pile. "I want you to open mine first."

I stare at the little lumps of glue that I've left drying inside my desk.

Mrs. Robertson glances at the clock. "Unfortunately, we won't have time," she says. "But I promise to open them at home."

I breathe a sigh of relief. This might be a real Christmas miracle. If I'm lucky, maybe the custodian will just sweep it away before she even knows it's from me. That way she won't think that I don't like her or that I'm not clever enough to give her a good present she deserves.

I gather the new snowman erasers we got and keep my eyes on the clock, praying, for once, for a speedy dismissal. Mrs. Robertson has flashed the lights, and we're all racing for our coats and backpacks, sugared up and excited for vacation.

The bell finally rings, and everyone cheers.

"Happy holidays, everyone!" Mrs. Robertson calls after us. The antlers she's wearing look a little lopsided. "Enjoy your time off."

I don't look at her or say good-bye. Instead, I keep my eyes down and zoom past her, ashamed, as I make a break for the metal doors.

41

★　★　★

I try my best to forget school during vacation.

I make snowmen with my downstairs neighbor, Sofia. I eat all the leftover *turrónes* from Abuela's *noche buena* dinner, even though Mami says those candies will rot my teeth. (What will she do then, I wonder darkly? Extract my teeth herself so we don't have to "waste money" at the dentist?) I watch cartoons and read and draw pictures with my old markers on New Year's Eve, thinking about the day when I'm grown and can buy all the mood rings and Chia Pets I want.

But soon, it's time to go back to school. I zip myself up into my old coat and slide my feet into the fake-fur-lined snow boots that Mami gave me for Christmas, one size too big so they'll last. The whole six blocks to school, I worry about my dumb present all over again. Maybe Mrs. Robertson won't like me anymore. Or maybe she'll think I'm cheap or just a plain weirdo. All I can think about is that silly half-naked lady.

I walk along the hall toward our room. Everything is so shiny and new at school after the holidays. The floors are polished, the desktops have been scoured, and all the bulletin boards have fresh paper on them.

"We have new seats," Mrs. Robertson tells us.

I breathe a sigh of relief. I'm at Table Two now, near the class library, far away from Charlene, who, I'm happy to find out, had the chicken pox over the whole break.

When I start to unpack my things, I see a white envelope inside my empty desk. My name is written across the front in

Mrs. Robertson's pretty script. I look over my shoulder to make sure no one is looking and open it slowly.

> *Dear Maria Elisa,*
>
>     *You were so kind to think of me at the holidays. How did you know that I always tear my stockings under the desk? It is so embarrassing! Thank you so much for finding an absolutely perfect gift for me. We can keep this our secret!*
>
> *Your friend,*
> *Mrs. Robertson*

I put the note inside my pocket and unpack my books. From under the desks, I check Mrs. Robertson's legs and smile. She's wearing pantyhose, and maybe they're the ones I gave her. Best of all, no one else knows. And just like that, my shame floats away, and everything inside me feels stronger and new.

# WHAT HAPPENED IN FOURTH GRADE

grew up in a rural area of upstate New York, and it was a good place to be.

Mostly.

Assuming you had the good fortune to fit in.

The elementary school I attended had originally been built as the high school for our small community. When the village built a new, very modern high school, the old school, with its high ceilings, enormous windows, and beautiful library, was converted into the elementary school.

Though I professed to hate school (it's a childhood obligation), I loved that old building. And just as well that I did, since I was there for six years, from first through sixth grade. The early grades were housed on the first floor, older grades ever higher, until in fifth and sixth grade we inhabited the top floor.

At that time it was common for schools to group kids by ability, rather than mixing things up, and I was lucky enough to be in the "top group." A few people moved in and out of the class as families came and went, but most of us were together, grade after grade, for six years.

We were a bright, funny, friendly group.

Mostly.

However, we were not as good as we thought we were, as I learned one afternoon in fourth grade.

That day our teacher, let's call her Mrs. Pike, sent one of our classmates, let's call him Andrew, on an errand to the office. Once he was safely out of the room, Mrs. Pike turned to us and said, "I didn't really need to have Andrew run that errand. The reason I sent him to the office is that I needed to talk to you." Pause. Meaningful and displeased look from our teacher, whom we loved. "Andrew's mother called me last night. She called to tell me that every afternoon when he comes home from school, he goes into his room and cries himself to sleep." Pause. "Because of the way you treat him."

An uneasy silence settled over the room.

How could this be? We were good kids, kind, not cruel.

Mostly.

Yet somehow our kindness had not extended to Andrew. He had been excluded from our friendship. Not bullied, not teased, not mocked. Just . . . cut out.

Why? Was it because of his bad teeth, some of them dark and craggy? Was it because we somehow sensed that, middle class as most of us were, his family was not quite at the same level as ours? Or was it simply because—and this was beyond our understanding at the time—someone always has to be the outsider, and one way groups bond is by shutting someone out?

More than fifty years later all I can tell you is that the memory of that afternoon burned itself into both my consciousness and my conscience.

I do not remember if I took immediate action. I think not likely. And though I don't remember exactly how it changed, I can tell you that by the time we were in high school, Andrew was my best friend.

Yet close as we became in those years, we never spoke of fourth grade and how he had been shut out.

Perhaps that was kindness on my part.

Or maybe it was kindness on his part, not reminding me of how things had been.

I know I never had the courage to bring it up.

But our teacher had the courage. She broke the silence and called us out on our behavior, on our cruelty.

And that's all it takes, I think, to snap the cycle of bullying. Even if—maybe especially if—the bullying is quiet and unintentional.

Truly, we didn't know how beastly we were being, we "good" kids. But our teacher had the strength, and the honesty, to tell us how our behavior was affecting one of our fellow students. To tell us what we were doing, and to try to stop it.

Which is exactly what a great teacher should do. Help you see what you are, and help you to be better.

So thank you, Mrs. Pike.

And, belatedly, my apologies to Andrew.

I never meant to hurt you.

# Bruce Coville

# THERE'S ALWAYS A GOAT

You know what makes me cranky?

Well, a lot of things, actually. But the thing I'm thinking of right now is finding out that I've been a butthead when I was thinking all along that I was a nice kid.

I mean, I *am* a nice kid, mostly. I don't pick on people. I'm kind to animals. I'd even help little old ladies cross the street, if I could find one who needed it. Most of the old ladies I know would probably clock me if I offered it.

And if you consider the fact that I'm a PK (Preacher's Kid), I'm especially nice, since we have a reputation of behaving badly to make up for all the goodness and light we get forced down our throats at home.

Of course, that's mostly hooey. My mom (she's the preacher in the family, my dad is a computer salesman) expects the three of us to behave and stay out of trouble, but she also knows we're gonna screw up on occasion and doesn't get all bent out of shape about it when we do. Mostly she just gives us The Look. And

47

believe me, when you get The Look from someone who is your mom and your minister all rolled into one, you know you've been Look-i-fied!

Anyway, here's what got me thinking about all this. There was this kid in my class who . . . well, let's say he wasn't the kind of kid who got invited to birthday parties.

It wasn't that the rest of us disliked him. We weren't mean to him, at least not actively. We all just kind of ignored him, without understanding how incredibly mean that could be. And, to be honest, I wouldn't have noticed or changed things if it hadn't been for this stupid Sunday School assignment I got last week.

Yes, of course I go to Sunday School. You think I have a choice?

Actually, I kind of like the class, mostly because our teacher, Mr. Hemsforth, is a pretty cool guy. He's a big Sherlock Holmes fan, and he likes to talk about observation and details. And last Sunday he cooked up an assignment that combined his Sherlock Holmes fanboyism with something kind of churchy.

"Here's what I want you to do this week," he said with his usual enthusiasm. "Pick out someone you don't know well and observe him or her closely. Learn something about your subject. But try not to let him or her know you're doing this. Pay attention! Notice details! And here's the important part: See if you can figure out something good you can do for that person without letting him or her know what you're up to."

We all groaned a little, of course, but that's just what you do when you get an assignment. I actually thought it sounded kind of interesting, and as I was walking home from church I tried to figure out who I should choose. I mean, most of the people around me I know at least medium well.

Then I thought of Stan Audibert. Stan was definitely the kid in our class I knew the least about. So on Monday I started observing him. I don't mean just watching him. Heck, we'd been in the same class for three years now, ever since his family moved to town in the middle of third grade. So I already knew that he was smart, had bad teeth, and sometimes smelled a little funny. But now I . . . well, I paid attention.

And the truth was, I didn't like what I saw.

I don't mean I didn't like what I saw about Stan. He didn't do anything wrong. What I didn't like was that hardly anyone said a thing to him for the entire day.

He didn't sit alone at lunch, but he might as well have. He was at the end of the table, and nobody paid any attention to him.

What was the reason for this?

When I thought about it, I realized I had hardly ever spoken to Stan myself. It wasn't that I disliked him. He had certainly never done anything bad to me.

It was then that I realized that our class had a kind of unspoken rule about Stan: *This is the guy we don't talk to.*

What the heck?!?

When we went outside for recess that day it was pretty much the same thing. Most of us have a set group of friends we hang out with. I'm a little different in that I tend to drift between two or three groups because I kind of like pretty much everyone.

Everyone but Stan?

I peeled off from my friends for a while and sat against the wall of the school. I had a paperback book I was pretending to read, but really it was Sherlock time. I was watching Stan and making mental notes.

He didn't hang out with anyone.

This situation was stranger than I had anticipated when I chose Stan to be the person I observed.

The next day, Tuesday, I decided to follow him home. Which makes me sound like a puppy or something, but the idea, of course, was to do it without being noticed. Very *un*puppylike.

The reason I could do it at all was that our town is pretty small, and if you live within a mile of the school, you're automatically a walker. Except by that year I was actually a biker, since I rode my bike to school most days. Even so, I was still called a walker.

Stan was a walker, too.

So now I was going to be a walker/stalker, which sounds kind of creepy. But I was just trying to learn about Stan and figure out how I could do something nice for him without him knowing what I was up to.

This assignment of Mr. Hemsforth's was turning out to be

trickier, and not only more interesting but also more troubling, than I had expected.

When the walkers were released that afternoon, I shot down to the bike rack and unlocked my bike. The rack is in the back of the school, and the walkers go out the front, so I wanted to get around fast enough to see which way Stan went.

But I was too slow and missed him. Dang!

The next day, Wednesday, I walked to school, figuring that way I would leave through the front entrance and could see where Stan was going. And if I was going to follow him, it probably made more sense to do so on foot, anyway.

I continued to watch Stan through the day, of course, and did notice one thing that I hadn't before. He liked comic books. Whenever he finished his work early, or had some free time, he would pull a comic book out of his desk and start reading it.

How had I not seen this before? I love comic books, too! I have a huge and nerd-tastic collection.

That afternoon I went out the front way and saw Stan turn left at the corner of Cherry and Main. I waited for a few minutes, then sprinted toward the corner and turned it.

Good! He was still in sight.

For the next several minutes I dawdled along a couple of blocks behind him. He didn't notice that I was following him, and why would he? As far as I could tell, nobody ever paid much attention to him. So why would he expect someone to be following him now?

I nearly lost him once, when he made two turns in a row, but other than that following him was easy. Finally he swung off into a driveway. We were in a not-very-good neighborhood now, and the house looked kind of run-down. I hurried forward in time to see that he didn't go inside. Instead he walked past the house and into the backyard, where there was a big tree. Pieces of wood had been nailed to the trunk, and I realized that they made a ladder. He had a tree house. Cool!

I waited for a while, trying to decide what to do. Finally I went to the ladder and started to climb. I was going to knock at the bottom of the tree house and say, "Anybody home?" I realized I was kind of breaking the rule for the assignment by doing that, but I had become more and more curious about Stan.

And now, as I write this down, I realize something else. I felt okay about doing that because we weren't in school, and no one would see me talking to him.

What the heck?!?

As it turned out, I didn't go all the way up to the tree house. I got about halfway on the ladder when I heard something strange. I stopped so I could listen more carefully. Then I knew what it was, and I felt sick to my stomach.

Stan was crying.

I couldn't go up there now, not out of the blue like this. If we had been friends it would be one thing, but we weren't. Because I'd never made the effort.

I wondered what he was crying about. There could be all kinds of things in his life worth crying over . . . when my dad got really sick last year I cried a lot, because I was so frightened. Or maybe Stan's puppy just died. But we wouldn't know that, would we, since none of us ever talked to him. Now that I was so aware of how lonely Stan must be, I couldn't help but think that he was probably crying because of how we had been treating him.

Even if that wasn't the reason, we certainly weren't doing anything to make the poor guy feel better about whatever was bothering him.

★ ★ ★

That night I couldn't sleep. I kept thinking about Stan, all alone all day, then crying in his tree house when he got home.

I felt disgusted with myself. Disgusted with all of us.

Finally I went down to my mother's study, where I knew she was working on her sermon for Sunday.

Her door was open, so I knocked on the frame. She looked up from her notes, surprised.

"Anything wrong, Bobby?" she asked.

I nodded.

"Well, come on in," she said. "Let's talk about it."

I sat in the big chair that my sibs and I call the confessional (even though we're not Catholic) because it's where we sit when we have to fess up to Mom about something that we've done. But I also sit there when I just need to talk to her.

I talked to her now about Stan, told her what I had seen, what I had heard that afternoon, and how puzzled I was that we had all cut him out so much.

When I was done she sighed and said, "Well, it sounds like your class has found its goat."

"Care to tell me what the heck that means?" I asked.

"It's a sad thing about humans," she said. "But there's almost always a goat, someone the group chooses to be the outside one. Calling that person the goat goes right back to the Bible. Here, let me see if I can find the right passage."

I expected her to go to the big Bible that sits on the wooden stand beside her desk. Instead she went to her laptop.

"If you know a few key words, Google can find the verse you're looking for in no time flat," she said, giving me a wink. "Ah, here we go! Leviticus sixteen, verse twenty-one: *And Aaron shall lay both his hands upon the head of the live goat, and confess over him all the iniquities of the children of Israel, and all their transgressions in all their sins, putting them upon the head of the goat, and shall send him away by the hand of a fit man into the wilderness.*

"That's called a *scapegoat*, Bobby. And people transfer not just their sins but their insecurities, their discomforts, and their fears onto the goat so they can feel better about themselves. We've been doing it for thousands of years. Only it's not usually a goat, which really wouldn't care. It's a human. As long as there is someone who doesn't fit in, someone to shut out, someone to be the 'goat,' everyone else feels more comfortable about him- or herself."

"That's awful!" I said.

"Yes, it is," said Mom. Then she looked me right in the eye

**54**

and said, "So . . . what are you going to do about it?"

Which is totally the way she operates.

I tossed and turned a lot that night, but by morning I had my plan.

I went downstairs to the family computer — which is separate from Mom's, which is sacred. It's not sacred because she writes her sermons on it. It's sacred because she would forget she is a minister and kill us all if anything happened to it.

After several drafts I had this invitation:

### Comic Book Swap

Bring your extra comics, any ones that you would like to trade, to class on Friday. During our TGIF free time at the end of the day, we'll meet at the back of the room for a swap fest! This could be a blast!

I posted it on the bulletin board where we put the Friday afternoon announcements for group meetings.

Then I handed copies of it to the five kids — three guys and two girls — who I knew were big comic book freaks.

And then I took one over to Stan's desk.

"Here," I said, handing it to him. "I noticed you like comic books. I hope you'll join us."

Stan looked at me, clearly surprised, a little puzzled.

Then he read the flyer.

And then he smiled.

★ ★ ★

I think Mr. Hemsforth will be pleased when I give my report on Sunday.

Truth is, it doesn't matter if he is or not.

I'm pretty sure I got it right.

And I feel better about myself than I have all week.

## Mike Winchell

# PRANKS GONE WRONG

**You've just spent forty minutes in** the classroom learning valuable information. Now you have a little time to kill between classes, and your friends are walking your way. This is *not* good. Hope you can stay out of trouble.

Authors Wendy Mass and Jacqueline West know about testing the rules. And their stories show that sometimes jokes can go a little too far at school.

WHAT REALLY HAPPENED

# PRANKS

Every year in mid-August I'd wait by the mailbox to see if that day's mail would bring my teacher assignment for the following school year. I couldn't wait to call my friends to find out if we were lucky enough to be in the same class. I had gotten lucky each year and never had to feel those first-day jitters without a good friend by my side. But my luck ran out in fifth grade.

My teacher assignment finally arrived that summer, and after a flurry of phone calls, I determined that I wouldn't have any of my friends in my fifth-grade class. Not a single one.

I was so upset that my mother took pity on me and called the school to see if she could get me transferred into another class. When that didn't work, she convinced them to give her a list of the other students in the class. That's how I learned that a girl named Amy who lived down the street was going to be my classmate.

Amy lived only about ten houses away, but it might as well have been ten states away for all that we had in common. She had three older brothers and was considered to be more worldly than the rest of us in our suburban late-seventies neighborhood. She knew all the curse words and had been to New York City *three times*! She laughed loud and long and didn't care what people thought of her. In all the years we'd lived so close, we hadn't said more than three words to each other.

Before school started that year, our mothers got us together, so we could bond, I guess. To my surprise, we *did* bond. Maybe it was because she was so close with her brothers, but I don't think she had other friends who were girls. Amy must have been as anxious as I was to have a friend in class. She quickly became the ringleader of our little twosome, and I was fine with that. She was fearless and bold, and when school started her friendship gave me confidence. I looked forward to school each day to see what new stunt she would come up with. We would hide bags of Lucky Charms cereal in our desks and nosh on them during class, when we weren't busy passing notes. We would make crank phone calls on the pay phone in the hallway, running away when the operator would call back. Then we got more daring.

Amy played the string bass at school, and the instrument was too big to travel with, so she could only practice at school. She was given the key to the band room in case she needed to get in there when the music teacher wasn't around. We realized it was a master skeleton key that would open many of the doors in the school, so of course Amy pocketed it. Owning the key made us feel powerful, like we had a big secret. It didn't work on our own classroom door, though, so we thought of a clever way to get in and out of our classroom when the door was locked at lunch.

We would make sure we were last in line to leave the classroom, and then we would stick a ruler up against the doorjamb so the door would look fully closed but really wasn't locked. We would later sneak back in and do little pranks, like moving people's desks, or leaving "secret admirer" love notes for various boys. Inevitably, we got caught. The teacher had alerted all the other kids to keep an eye out for how the culprits were getting in, so basically twenty kids were set on our trail. One boy saw Amy place the ruler in the door as we left one day for lunch and alerted the teacher—loudly! The teacher didn't formally punish us; I guess she figured severe embarrassment was good enough. She also moved our desks to opposite sides of the room. After school we wrote a letter together, promising always to be friends and never to let the spirit of our adventures fade away. Then we burned it and put the ashes in a sandwich bag that we buried under a flat stone near the driveway of Amy's house. We promised we'd dig it up together one day.

Twenty years later, I went alone to the house that was no longer Amy's. The bag was gone. No doubt some unknowing landscaper had swept it away.

# Wendy Mass

## THE STORY

# STORIES UNDER STONES

*efresh . . . refresh . . . refresh . . . refresh . . .*

Mom stands behind me as I hit the Enter key repeatedly. I've been hitting it pretty much nonstop since nine this morning, and it's almost noon.

"Abby, you're going to break the keyboard if you keep beating up on it like that," Mom says gently. She knows I'm nervous. I've waited all summer to find out which of my friends I'll be in class with this year. The lists are supposed to be posted on the school's website today. I don't have a big group of friends like some kids. I've heard Mom tell other moms that I'm still "coming into myself," whatever that means. I don't even care which teacher I get. There are only four fifth-grade classes, so I'm bound to have at least a few friends in my class; the question is who. I'm hoping it's Suzy and Samantha, but I'll be happy if it's Maya or Kimmy. Or even any of the girls from last year's Girl Scout troop or my dance class.

*Refresh . . . refresh . . . refresh . . .* hurrah!

It's up! The list is up! My heart is already thumping fast and now it starts to pound against my chest. Mom leans over as I scroll down the page. Ms. Smithy's class is first. I scan the alphabetical list of names. Since my last name starts with a *B*, I quickly see that mine isn't there. Samantha's is, though. And Kimmy's. Next is Mr. Parlo's class. Maya, Janie from Girl Scouts, and Brin from tap lessons. Not me. Next is Mrs. Kaine. Four girls from Girl Scouts, and Suzy. Plus Alexis and Becca from my class last year, who I was just starting to know! I'm beginning to panic. I can't think of any more friends! Mom puts her hand on my shoulder as I scroll down to the last class. Ms. Lions. There I am. My eyes dart through the rest of the list, but they soon get too clouded with tears to see straight. I push the chair away from the computer and stand up. Mom moves to hug me, but I just stand there.

"It can't be that bad," Mom says. "I'm sure you know some nice kids in there. And Ms. Lions is supposed to be wonderful."

"I know their names," I tell her through my tears. "But they're not my friends. Who am I even going to sit with at lunch? Can you call the school and ask them to change my class?"

She frowns. "You know I can't do that. They only let you request a change for a really good reason. Like your teacher is your aunt. Or you need to be kept away from a particular child in the class. You've never had any problems with any of the kids, have you?"

I search my brain to come up with something. "Jimmy Henkins broke my crayon in first grade and lied about it, and I got in trouble. Is that good enough?"

She sighs and strokes my hair. "I'm afraid not, honey. I'm sure there's someone in the class that you'll click with. Let's look at the list."

I sulk my way back over to the computer. "Here," Mom says, pointing to the name right below me on the list. "Madeline Bennett. She lives right around the corner, can't be more than ten houses away. She must be on your bus, right?"

I shake my head. "One of her brothers drives her. He's in high school." How can I explain to my mom that Madeline Bennett isn't an appropriate friend? She hangs around with high school kids, and we're not even in middle school yet. And I heard one of her brothers paid her fifty cents to curse in front of this little first grader. I can't tell Mom any of this, so I run upstairs instead. I don't even bother to grab my phone, which my parents finally agreed to give me this summer. I don't want to read my friends' texts telling me how excited they are to be with so-and-so and what an awesome year it's gonna be.

I have two more weeks before school starts, and I plan to spend it moping around and feeling sorry for myself. I make it two days doing exactly that before my mom knocks on the door and announces that we're going to the Bennetts' house so Madeline and I can "get to know each other."

I stare at her. "But I don't want to be friends with her. I told you that."

"No, you didn't," she argues. "You only said she's not on your bus."

Well, I guess technically that's true. "Please don't make me do this. It's going to be really weird. We've never even spoken to each other."

"Eat your cereal and then I'll walk you over. If it's awful after two hours, text me and I'll come get you."

"Fine," I grumble. "I guess I don't have anything better to do."

"That's the spirit!" she says, hitting me playfully on the arm.

As soon as we arrive, Madeline grabs me by the arm and takes me to her room. We play a bunch of games, and she has a whole stash of candy hidden inside a toy cash register. When I ask her where all the candy came from, she says she stole it. Then she winks at me. My eyes widen.

I'm hooked.

Two hours come and go, and I don't even think about texting Mom. I'm having too much fun. Madeline's house is totally different from mine. Mine is quiet — it's just Mom, Dad, me, and our cat, Hector. Dad's the come-home-from-the-office-and-settle-in-to-read-and-relax type, and Hector is so old that he doesn't move much from his little cat bed. Madeline's house has different music blasting out of each room, along with two boys and two dogs running everywhere. Bright, colorful paintings and black-and-white photographs cover the walls; soft rugs dot the floors in every room. And everyone laughs a lot. Sure, we laugh at my house, but here everyone has these big booming laughs, even Madeline.

"I should probably go," I finally say. We'd been exploring the brook behind her house for hours, pretending to be pirates hiding treasure. The slope was pretty steep, and the water was kind of high, but she said she was allowed to go down there. I'm not so sure I believed her, and her parents weren't home to ask. I didn't push it, though, because I really wanted to do it.

"I'll walk you back," she says, pulling two thorns out of the palm of her hand and sucking on the blood. This girl is fearless. Maybe some of it will rub off on me.

I discover that Madeline's family always goes away to the beach the week before school, so I don't see her again until I step into Ms. Lions's class. On the whiteboard is a giant image of a lion in the jungle. Coming out of its mouth is a big speech bubble that says "Sit anywhere you like."

I freeze. No teacher has let us choose our own seats before! Kids begin pouring into the room, and I start feeling that same dread I'd felt when I first saw the class list on the computer. I really, *really*, don't know anyone. Kids are choosing seats left and right, and I'm still just standing, frozen.

Then Madeline flies in right as the bell rings, and I can breathe again. She grabs me and leads me to the last two desks in the back row, the only ones still empty. She tosses me a little Baggie filled with Every Flavor Jelly Beans, which we're definitely not supposed to have in class. She has a matching bag. "To nosh on during the day," she whispers and sticks hers deep into her empty desk. I quickly do the same.

Ms. Lions takes attendance, and when she reads our two names and we say, "Here," and start giggling, she says, "Guess I'm going to have to keep an eye on you two," which only makes us giggle more. An hour later I crack up when Madeline scrunches up her whole face and says, "Earwax flavor! Watch out for that one!" I've never known anyone like her.

One morning when Ms. Lions is busy writing on the board, Madeline passes me a note, folded up and taped around the edges. I stick my hands inside the desk to unwrap it. When I get it open, a long skinny key falls out! I glance up to make sure Ms. Lions didn't hear it clatter, then I quickly read the note.

*The music teacher lent me this key so I could*
*use the music room during lunch to practice for*
*the performance next week. After you finish eating*
*today, get a bathroom pass and come join me.*
*I have a plan. PS: When you're finished reading*
*this note, rip it up and eat it!*

I slip the key back to her then rip up the note. Hopefully she was kidding about the eating-it part.

It takes longer than I'd hoped to get the bathroom pass at lunchtime, because only one girl and one boy can be gone at a time. When I finally make it down to the music room, Madeline is the only person there. I stand at the door and watch her play what looks like a giant violin turned upside down. She's really getting into it, pushing the big bow back and forth across the strings with her whole body. I can't say that it makes the world's most pleasant noise, though, and I'm not exactly sorry when she sees me and lifts the bow off the strings.

"Yo!" she says. She closes the music book and stashes the bow in a narrow box on the floor. "So here's the scoop. That key is, like, a skeleton key, which means it should work in any lock in the building. Haven't you always wondered what was actually in the janitor's closet?"

"Um . . . not really?"

She frowns. "Okay, bad example. What if it opened our own

**66**

classroom door and we could steal next week's math test! I know Ms. Lions copies them a week early and puts them in her bottom desk drawer."

"Um, sure," I say, my stomach twisting up a bit. I'm hoping she's just talking but doesn't really mean it. But then she says, "Cool, let's go now!"

"Now?" I ask, my stomach twisting further. "Shouldn't we plan it out a little more? Like, you know, watch the hallway for a while to make sure the coast is clear?"

"We can do that when we get up there." Without waiting for an answer, she heads out of the room. I have no choice but to follow. We hurry up the stairs and peek around the corner. No one is in our wing of the hallway. "The coast is clear," she whispers, sounding like a spy in a movie.

"There's only five minutes till recess is over," I whisper.

"Plenty of time," Madeline says, pulling at the doorknob. It's locked, as we knew it would be. The last person out of the room at lunchtime has the job of closing the door behind them, and it locks automatically. The teacher is the only one with the key. Glancing both ways again to make sure no one's around, Madeline slips the key into the lock and twists. Nothing happens. She pulls the key out, pushes it back in, and turns again. Still nothing.

I let out the breath I didn't realize I was holding. I'm relieved, but say only, "Oh well."

Madeline gives one more good yank on the doorknob. "Okay. Plan B," she says.

"There's a Plan B?" I ask warily.

She nods. "Janitor's closet."

Plan B worked. I have a carton of industrial-size green sponges hidden under my bed to prove it.

I'd hoped Madeline's dreams of breaking into our classroom had faded, but a week later she slips me another note:

*When it's time to leave for lunch, we need to be*

*last in line. PS: Rip and eat.*

This time I just crumple up the note. Then I think better of it and rip it into pieces. I may not be a master spy, but I know better than to leave written evidence.

When the bell rings for lunch, Madeline and I exchange a glance and take our time gathering our lunch bags. Soon it's only the two of us left. Madeline waves me ahead, and then just before the door swings closed behind her, her hand darts out and wedges something in the doorjamb. The door still shuts.

"What is that?" I ask.

"A ruler," she says. "It keeps the little lock thingy from going into the wall."

I have to admit this is very clever. The door really looks fully closed. When we get to the cafeteria, Madeline gets her usual pass to the music room and I take the bathroom one. It's a good thing the lunchroom aides change all the time or they'd start to think I have a bladder problem!

The door opens just like Madeline said it would. We slip inside, taking the ruler with us. Madeline runs over to the teacher's desk and opens the bottom drawer. "It's not here!" she says, frowning.

"Oh, well," I say, trying to make my face look disappointed.

She shuts the drawer. "We can't just leave without doing anything."

I look around the room. "We can move people's desks around," I suggest. That seems pretty harmless.

"Nice!" Madeline says, and we get to work. I decide to move my own desk, too, since it would look obvious if everyone else's was moved but ours. Madeline suddenly stops and grabs her notebook from her own desk. "I have an even better idea," she says. "Who do you think is the cutest boy in our class?"

At the same time we both answer, "Ashton!"

She rips out a blank page and writes:

*Dear Ashton,*

*I think you're really cute. Will you go out with me?*

*Your true love,*

*Emily*

I put my hand over my mouth. Emily is the shyest girl in our class. I don't think I've ever heard her speak unless Ms. Lions called on her. Madeline grabs a piece of tape off the teacher's desk and tapes the note right on the back of Ashton's chair!

We hurry out of the room, trying not to laugh. It's a good thing there's only fifteen more minutes of lunch left, because I'm too nervous and excited to eat. As we file into the classroom I prepare to look surprised. Turns out I don't have to prepare anything! My jaw falls open when I step inside and see all of the desks are back exactly where they were! Before either of us can accuse the other of doing it, Ms. Lions says, "Madeline and Abby,

**69**

you're wanted in the principal's office." The class turns to look at us, and a few kids say, "Ooooo" and "You're in trouble!"

So it turns out the hallways have cameras in them. We were spotted breaking into the classroom and the janitor's closet. We both have to do chores around the school for the next month. I'm also grounded.

My mom says that Madeline is a bad influence, and maybe she's right. Maybe (probably) I should have told her that sneaking around school wasn't a good idea and that I didn't really want to do it. But Madeline is the first best friend I've ever had. And even after the embarrassment of getting caught, I have to admit I miss the freedom and power that the key and the ruler gave us. What if I never have another partner in crime who needs me as much as I need her?

As soon as our punishments are lifted, I go over to her house again. Since our lives as mischief-makers are over, we decide to write a short story instead about two girls who become super-famous spies and live lives of romance and excitement as they travel the globe. We print it out and then burn it. We put the ashes in a sandwich Baggie and bury it under a flat stone in front of Madeline's house. We promise each other we'll come back as grown-ups and dig it up and remember the crazy things we did together in fifth grade. Maybe by that time there will be a burned-up story hidden under each stone on the path.

I hope so.

# Jacqueline West

# THE EDIBLE LIE DETECTOR

There's a line between *pretending* and *lying*.

Growing up, I wasn't always sure where that line was. It seemed to be a pretty blurry, wavery line, anyway. I drifted over it several times a day. Usually I drifted inside my own head, where the things I pretended most intently had turned into things I truly believed—like that I was due to unearth a triceratops skeleton in our backyard sandbox any day now, or that our laundry chute was a passage to Wonderland, or that the food in our fridge came to life every time we closed the door.

I was happy in my pretend world. But because I also lived in the real world, surrounded by real family and real classmates and real teachers, the line between *pretending* and *lying* eventually drifted out of my head into reality.

One morning in third grade, as Miss Miller wrote on the blackboard, I decided to pretend I was falling asleep.

I'd practiced this often—sometimes I was Sleeping Beauty with the spindle; sometimes I was in the field of poppies in *The*

*Wizard of Oz*—so I knew just what to do. I let my eyelids slide shut and my head droop onto my arms, and made my breathing slow. In a few seconds, I almost believed I *was* asleep.

"Jacqui?" I heard Miss Miller say. "Jacqui?"

I didn't move. The classroom grew quiet.

Miss Miller's footsteps tapped closer to my desk. "Jacqui, it's time to wake up."

I waited until Miss Miller gave my shoulder a gentle shake. Then I raised my head, blinking groggily, pretending—or maybe believing—I'd just remembered where I was. There were giggles all around.

"Well, that's the first time a student has fallen asleep on me!" said Miss Miller, laughing too. "Now, back to state capitals..."

As class resumed, I sat at my desk, a sparkling thrill racing through me. *It had worked.* I'd made Miss Miller stop teaching. I'd made the room go silent. I'd made believe I was asleep, and I'd made everyone else believe it, too.

The power! *The possibilities!*

A few weeks later, I raised the stakes.

It was the chilly midwinter. We bundled up for recess, keeping warm by playing tag on the hard-packed playground snow. Conditions were perfect for my next act.

I'd never broken a bone, but I thought it looked extremely exciting. People in books were always using crutches—Clara from *Heidi*, Tiny Tim, Pollyanna—and I'd spent hours hobbling around with two croquet mallets under my arms, wishing for crutches of my own. So, the next time someone yelled

"Go!" I took off, let my boots skid, and flopped over into the snow.

"My ankle . . . ," I whimpered from the icy drifts. ". . . I can't move it."

My classmates rushed off to get the playground monitors, and I lay there, watching puffs of breath freeze on my hair. I should have been freezing, too, but it was surprisingly easy to keep still. In fact, the longer I waited, the more certain I was that a throbbing pain had settled in my right ankle. Soon I couldn't have climbed out of the snow if a herd of velociraptors was barreling toward me.

A crowd of boots crunched closer.

"You're sure you can't get up?" said an adult voice from above.

"I'm sure," I whispered. And it was almost *not* a lie.

The monitors locked their hands behind my back and under my knees, lifted me up in this floating chair, and carried me to the nurse's office.

There weren't many places I liked better than Nurse Nelson's office. That afternoon, I got to sit in one of her comfy chairs, wrapped with one of her special ice packs, and after an hour or so, I bravely returned to class, practicing my very best limp all the way.

The only thing better than Nurse Nelson's office was getting sent home from it.

Staying home from school meant lying on the couch, sipping soda, and pretending to be a delicate invalid, like Beth in *Little*

*Women* or Colin in *The Secret Garden*. And pretending to be sick was easy: No external evidence was required. It was so easy, in fact, that I did it *all the time*. I'd had everything from imaginary migraines to imaginary appendicitis.

The problem was that my mother—who knew my make-believe tendencies better than anyone—was getting pretty hard to fool.

This seemed unfair. If I pretended something until I truly *believed* it, shouldn't other people believe *me*? If I believed in a lie, was it even a lie anymore? Not according to that blurry line in my brain.

One school day that spring, after imagining stomachaches until my stomach actually ached, I raised a shaky hand. "Miss Miller?" I croaked. "I think I might have the flu . . ."

Nurse Nelson said she'd call my mother. Then she left me in one of her comfy chairs, feeling almost sick and very pleased with myself.

After several minutes, there was a tap at the door.

It wasn't my mom.

Instead, my classmate Stella stepped inside. "I brought these for my birthday." She held a Tupperware box under my nose. "You could take one for when you feel better. They're homemade chocolate cupcakes with cream filling, just like the Hostess ones."

I tried pretending to be too nauseous to care, but the smell of chocolate and the twirls of white icing called out to me. Delicately, I picked up a cupcake.

"Thank you," I whispered as Stella backed out again.

I put the cupcake in my lap. For a few minutes, the cake and I stared at each other. Its frosting glistened. My mouth started to water. The seconds ticked past on the big white wall clock.

Finally, I lifted the cupcake and took a nibble of the edge, where it wouldn't show. It was soft and delicious and utterly unsatisfying. I waited a few more seconds. Then I took a nibble of the other edge.

I knew I should stop. I should imagine I didn't want the cupcake, but I couldn't—not when I knew that gooey filling waited inside, a hidden trove of whipped white sugar . . .

And that was how my mother found me sitting in the nurse's office, pretending to be sick to my stomach, with my tongue stuck inside a chocolate cupcake.

I didn't make anyone else believe me that day.

# THE TROLL TRUTH

The troll thing began when Sean moved to town.

Asha and Sean were in different classes—she was in Miss Ferry's, and he was in Mr. Griffin's—but the school was small enough that everyone knew the new kid's name.

Asha also knew that, after her, Sean was the slowest eater in the whole fifth grade. After four lunchtimes in a row when the two of them had been the last kids in the cafeteria, Asha picked up the remains of her sandwich and sidled cautiously toward the boy's table.

The new kid had light blond hair that seemed to stick up with permanent static electricity. Up close, Asha could see a splash of pale freckles across the bridge of his nose. He was nibbling a strip of string cheese. In front of him, other bits of food were lined up in a row: one apple slice, a single cracker, a lone gummy bear.

"Why do you leave a tiny bit of everything?" asked Asha, who always chewed her sandwich into strange shapes, and who appreciated other forms of creative eating.

Sean glanced around. Then he leaned toward Asha, his eyes intent. "For the trolls," he whispered.

A telltale spark of excitement ran up the back of Asha's neck. It was the spark that meant an imagining game—her favorite kind of game—was about to begin.

"The school trolls," she said. "Of course."

"Want to help leave it for them?" Sean asked.

"Sure." Asha stuffed the last bite of Florida-shape sandwich into her mouth and hurried after Sean onto the playground.

They found a spot close to the school wall, sheltered by a low, thick hedge. "This is good," said Asha. "It's out of sight—"

"—but not far away," Sean finished. "Trolls don't like to be outdoors for long. At least, not when they're aboveground."

"Right," said Asha. "That's why they live in big old buildings, like schools."

Of course, Asha didn't *know* that trolls lived in big old buildings. But her imagination bubbled with ideas so clear they seemed like facts—and as soon as something *seemed* like a fact, Asha had no trouble believing it. In her imagination, the fireflies blinking above her misty backyard were teeny fairies that only transformed into insects when a human got too close. (Fact: Fairies had a keen sense of smell for humans.) Her imagination was sure that the neighbors' German shepherd turned into a werewolf during the full moon, so Asha gave it treats and belly rubs to keep on its good side. (Another fact: Even werewolves loved belly rubs.) She'd had plenty of practice imagining things on her own, but it was thrilling to combine her imaginings with someone else's. It made everything twice as real.

"I'll get some stones," Sean offered.

"Ones that aren't too big," said Asha. "It's a fact that most trolls are pretty small."

They arranged several handfuls of small, flat stones against the school's brick wall. Sean made a little stone table, and Asha covered it with a layer of pretty yellow leaves. (Fact: Trolls loved the color yellow.) Finally, and precisely, they placed the food on top.

"I think the trolls will like it," said Asha.

Sean gave a satisfied nod. "The important thing is that now they won't play any of their tricks on *us*."

Asha and Sean also happened to take the same bus home. They spent that afternoon's ride huddled in a green vinyl seat, discussing what kinds of tricks trolls might play.

They agreed that trolls were to blame whenever your favorite pencil disappeared. Trolls also stole erasers, library books, and Legos, and they used these things to build their villages inside the school's heating vents. If they were angry, trolls would mess up your desk or even take your finished homework. Trolls *hated* troll dolls—they found their puffy hairstyles insulting—and they played tricks on teachers by switching their regular coffee for decaf, which was why teachers were sometimes so inexplicably crabby.

It all made perfect sense to Asha.

The next afternoon, when Asha and Sean hurried out to the

playground, the food they'd left for the trolls was gone. The little stone table was gone, too, so they rebuilt it. They covered it with a baby carrot, a piece of sandwich chewed into the shape of a squirrel, and one Oreo cookie.

Just before the bell rang, Sean reached out and broke the cookie in half.

Asha gasped.

"I'm just taking half," Sean argued preemptively, through a mouthful of chocolate crumbs.

A prickle of excited fear raced up Asha's neck. "They're going to be *mad*," she warned.

When Sean rushed toward her on the bus a few hours later, whispering that his best sparkly Teenage Mutant Ninja Turtle pencil had just disappeared from his desk, Asha wasn't surprised. Deep down, she knew that Sean had probably lost the pencil in some perfectly ordinary way. But imagining that Oreo-hungry trolls had stolen it was much more fun.

★ ★ ★

It was also fun to spend the dull parts of each school day doodling troll portraits in order to compare them on the bus ride home. Sean and Asha concluded that trolls — even girl trolls — had no hair, but Sean thought they usually dressed in overalls, while Asha believed they wore something more like long underwear. They both began keeping special troll notebooks, diagramming troll villages built of pencils and lost homework, and making lists of collected troll facts. It was the most exciting school project Asha had ever done.

One afternoon, while Asha and Sean were arguing over whether trolls wore boots or went barefoot, Curt Reiss flopped over the green vinyl bus seat right in front of them.

"What are you two talking about?" he demanded.

Curt had the loudest voice of any kid in the fifth grade. When he recited the Pledge of Allegiance, you could hear him from one end of the school to the other. Plus, he was big; he could swing across the playground monkey bars with his toes still touching the ground. He was used to being listened to.

Sean's mouth clamped shut.

Asha tried to keep hers shut, too. But Curt loomed over her like an inflating hot-air balloon, seeming to grow larger with each passing second. Finally, Asha couldn't take it anymore.

"Trolls," she blurted.

Sean's elbow jabbed her in the side. He pointed to a line in Asha's open notebook: *Fact: Trolls don't like being talked about to anyone who doesn't believe in them.*

"Trolls?" Curt repeated, in his gigantic voice. "Like those little frizzy-haired dolls?"

"No," muttered Asha. "Not like that."

Curt yanked the notebook out of her hands. He studied her portrait of a bald, bootless, long-underweared troll. "Huh," he said. Then he dropped the notebook into her lap and turned away.

Asha felt a rush of relief. Curt could have drawn the whole bus's attention. He could have stolen her notebook. This hadn't been so bad, really.

She turned toward Sean.

He was staring at her, his eyes wide and his lips tight. "You *really* shouldn't have done that," he whispered.

★ ★ ★

Asha woke up for school the next morning feeling as though she'd spent the night being bitten by imaginary mosquitoes: itchy and irritated and underrested. As usual, her curly brown hair was a mess of morning tangles, but when she stumbled into the bathroom, Asha saw that they weren't just tangles. They were knots. Hundreds of tiny knots, as though someone with very small, precise fingers had tied each one. It took her ages to comb half of them out, and by the time she got downstairs, she could only grab an un-toasted Pop-Tart before finding her backpack and rushing out the door.

She was standing at the bus stop, her hands in her coat pockets, when her fingers brushed a scrap of paper.

Asha pulled the paper out.

It was a tiny folded note. A message in shaky pencil-drawn letters was scrawled across one side: *STOP TAAKING ABOWT US*.

Invisible frost covered Asha's skin.

The trolls had heard her speak to Curt. They had followed her home, into her bedroom. They had tied knots in her hair and left this note in her pocket.

*Wait*, Asha told herself. As fun as it was to believe in them, she *knew* that trolls were imaginary. It had to have been someone else.

"For creatures that live in a school, they aren't very good spellers," said Sean, when Asha sat down beside him on the bus, holding out the note with shaky fingers.

"But it was really *you*, wasn't it?" Asha whispered. "You were sitting beside me. You heard me talk to Curt. You could have slipped the note into my pocket."

Sean looked genuinely confused. "It wasn't me," he insisted. "I swear."

Asha swallowed. She turned away, staring out the bus windows into the dim fall morning.

Maybe Sean *had* written the note, and he was just a good pretender. Or maybe he believed that Asha had written the note herself, adding to the game. She tried to run her fingers through her still-tangly hair. But who had sneaked into her bedroom in the middle of the night?

Just to be safe, Asha decided to leave the trolls an extra large portion of her lunch that day.

★ ★ ★

Asha and Sean were crouched beside the wall in their usual spot that afternoon, rebuilding the stone table, when a shadow rippled over them.

"Hey!" said a voice.

Asha and Sean whipped around. Mr. Browney, the school custodian, stood right behind them.

"So you two are the ones leaving food here," he said, pointing his leaf rake toward the telltale table, where a slice of cheese, a strawberry, and a sandwich chewed into the shape of a tuba were waiting. "You can't keep doing this, kids. It draws rodents and insects, and it could rot. It's not sanitary."

Sean and Asha exchanged an anxious look.

"Why are you doing it?" Mr. Browney asked. "Are you feeding wild animals?"

"No," said Asha.

"Are you playing house?"

"No," said Sean, sounding offended.

"Then—what?" Mr. Browney waited, looking back and forth between them.

Asha couldn't meet Mr. Browney's eyes, but she could feel the weight of them on her, making her face flush and her stomach squirm.

Sean must have been feeling the same thing, because he suddenly muttered—

"Trolls."

"What?" said Mr. Browney.

Asha glanced at Sean, who was staring down at the toes of his blue Converse sneakers. Under his freckles, his face was bright red.

"Trolls live in the school," Asha said, turning back to Mr. Browney. "In the walls."

"Hmm." Mr. Browney's mouth twitched. "Well . . . I need you not to leave any more troll food out here, or *anywhere* except the cafeteria. Agreed?"

"Agreed," Sean and Asha whispered.

When the bell rang, they both shuffled indoors, unable to look at each other.

Asha had gym class that afternoon. Everyone had to change clothes for the mile run, and afterward, they all trooped sweatily back to the basement locker room.

Asha was not only the slowest eater in her grade but the slowest dresser. It took her several minutes to find both socks and then to tie her shoes, and by the time she stood up and looked around, the rest of the class had already made it out the door. As she started to follow them, there was a soft *click*.

The lights snapped out.

Total blackness surrounded her.

"I'm still in here!" Asha called. "Hello!"

There was no answer.

Asha groped toward the door, pawing desperately at the darkness until her hands had closed around the metal door handle. She wrenched it to one side.

The door didn't budge.

Asha tried again, pulling the handle as hard as she could, but the door clearly wasn't just stuck. It was locked.

An icy, awful feeling poured through Asha's body. She pounded on the door with both fists, screaming, "Help! *Help!*" until both hands ached and she could barely breathe.

And while she stood there, gasping, from somewhere in the deep and quiet darkness came a sound.

Asha whirled around, pressing her back to the door.

It was a rustling sound. A *scurrying* sound.

It was the sound of dozens of small bodies crawling out through the vents in the walls, swarming through the darkness . . .

. . . marching straight toward her.

Asha had just opened her mouth to scream when the door

**84**

behind her flew open. She staggered backward, right into Mr. Browney's arms.

"The trolls!" Asha panted, trying to peer back into the locker room's darkness. "They were there. They — "

"Right. The trolls again," Mr. Browney interrupted. "Come with me." Keeping one hand on Asha's shoulder, he led her upstairs to the counselor's office.

There, seated in the counselor's waiting room, with his hair looking exceptionally staticky and his face very pale under its freckles, was Sean.

Asha grabbed the arms of Sean's chair. "Did you just lock me in the locker room and turn out the lights because I told Mr. Browney about the trolls?" she demanded.

"What? No!" Sean looked shocked. "Did you just destroy everything in my entire desk because *I* told Mr. Browney about the trolls?"

"How *could* I have?" Asha exploded. *"I was stuck in the basement locker room!"*

At that moment, the door swung open. Mr. Alph, the guidance counselor, stood on the threshold, looking down at them with his kind brown eyes.

"Sean. Asha." Mr. Alph nodded at them both. "I think we need to have a talk."

★ ★ ★

The bus ride home was quieter than usual.

Asha and Sean left their troll notebooks in their bags. They sat side by side for a while, not looking at each other.

85

At last, Sean said, "What are you going to do with your notebook?"

Asha sighed. "I think I'll stick it in the back of my closet. Under the stack of itchy sweaters. What about you?"

"I don't know. Maybe I'll hide mine in the basement, so it will be easier to forget about it."

"Mr. Alph was probably right," said Asha. "We mixed up pretending with lying. And we let our imaginations run away with us."

Sean gave her a look. "Is that what you really think?"

"That's what I really think. Probably."

"But if you *believe* something is true, then you're not lying."

"Yeah. I guess so." Asha paused. "Maybe something can be true even if it isn't real."

They both gazed out the window for a minute.

"Well . . . ," said Sean softly, "*I* think Mr. Alph might be covering things up, for reasons of his own." He met Asha's eyes. "Haven't you noticed his name? Mr. *Alph*? It sounds almost like—"

"Shh," whispered Asha. Excitement began to buzz in her stomach. She glanced around, making sure nobody else was listening. Then she pulled out her notebook and flipped to a fresh page. ". . . And did you notice how *pointy* his ears are?"

# CLASS PROJECTS

**It's school project time. Now is your** chance to show off some creativity and imagination—a way to stand out from your classmates.

Bruce Hale and Sarah Prineas know how important class projects can be. And they know that sometimes those projects can inspire others—or even get a little out of control.

# Bruce Hale

# MAGICAL THINKING:
## THE GREAT HOMEWORK EXPERIMENT

'm not sure how I first got the idea. Maybe I misinterpreted a sarcastic comment from an older kid, maybe I came up with the inspiration myself. But somehow, in second grade, I decided that homework was optional.

Our teacher, Miss Peters, made a big deal over homework the first time she introduced the concept to us. She impressed on us how grown-up we were becoming, getting to do homework like the older kids. After all, the kindergartners didn't have it; neither did the first-graders. But we second-graders did.

At this point I thought, if I'm grown-up enough to do homework, I'm grown-up enough to choose not to. It never occurred to me to ask Miss Peters her opinion.

(In my defense, let me say that lots of my classmates engaged in other kinds of magical thinking. My friend Toni, for example, still believed in the Easter Bunny.)

As the first weeks of the school year unfolded, the Great Homework Experiment began. I approached it like a true scientist. Each time Miss Peters handed out assignments, I accepted mine cheerfully, lifted the wooden lid of my desk, and shoved the homework inside, never to be seen again. (Scientists always try to be consistent so their results can be repeated.)

Gradually the homework accumulated in that dark, hidden space, along with random playground treasures—an interesting rock, someone's lost army toy—and a few less-than-thrilling items from my sack lunches. (Dried apricots, anyone? Anyone?)

A month slipped by. My experiment was progressing nicely. The homework was now as thick and deep as a drift of snow, and I had to dig through it to find my treasures. A small inconvenience for the good of science.

Clearly, I wasn't thinking this whole experiment through—that eventually I'd run out of desk space and I'd have to do something about all these assignments. But that was the future, and I was living in the present.

Now it also never occurred to me that my parents and my teacher might communicate. But wouldn't you know it? That was exactly what happened.

A little over a month into the new school year, Miss Peters announced Back to School Night. Our parents would be visiting our classroom for the first time. A faint sense of dread wriggled in my belly, but I stuffed it down and tried to ignore it, just like the homework.

The night arrived, and my parents showed up. They oohed and ahhed over my art pieces on the wall. They heard about my excellent tetherball skills. And then the subject came up.

"You know," Miss Peters said, "Bruce doesn't seem to be turning in his homework. Is he leaving it at home?"

"Homework, what homework?" my parents asked. "He tells us he never has any."

Everyone looked at me. I tried on a smile. It wilted.

Busted.

I knew that great scientists accept great risks. But now it looked like my experiment was in jeopardy.

At this point, we all walked over to my desk. "Open it up," said Miss Peters.

I gulped and obeyed her command. Inside my desk, practically filling the cavity, was a massive wad of paper: all the assignments I'd been ignoring for the past month.

My dad turned his gimlet eye on me, the look he gave when he wanted you to know he was deadly serious about what he was going to say. He said, "There are going to be some changes made."

And somehow I knew that my brief scientific career had ended. The Great Homework Experiment, along with the era of magical thinking, was over.

# Bruce Hale

## EGBERTO FRANKENSTEIN

No fourth-grader had ever won the science fair before, and Egberto Cruz knew why. Their projects were boring with a capital *B*. The Water Cycle, How to Make a Lemon Battery, Pinto Bean Germination, and How Does Frost Form were some of the most interesting.

And that was being generous.

"I'm going to change all that," Egberto told his friend Robbie at recess.

"Change what?" said Robbie. "Your shorts?" Robbie could always be counted on for the classy jokes.

"I'm going to be the first fourth-grader at this school to win the science fair," said Egberto, retrieving the soccer ball.

"Dream on, dude," said Robbie. "You know Maya's already got it in the bag."

Maya Jackson, sixth-grade genius, had been winning science fairs since she was in second grade at a school across town. She'd continued her unbroken string of victories when she transferred to Rupert Munch Elementary a year ago. Everybody knew she'd sweep this year's science fair.

Everybody but Egberto.

He bounced the ball from knee to knee. "She can be beaten," he said.

"By Albert Einstein maybe," said Robbie. "But he's dead."

Egberto shook his head. "By me. All I need is the right project."

What he didn't mention was that winning the science fair was crucial. Since he was currently conducting a "no homework" experiment, Egberto's entire science grade depended on his project doing well at the fair.

The ball went flying, and Robbie chased it. "What are you gonna do," he asked, "cure cancer? Create life? Build a time machine?"

A funny look spread over Egberto's face. "What did you just say?"

"Build a time machine?"

"No, before that."

Robbie's eyebrows rose. "Create life? I was joking."

Nodding slowly, Egberto said, "Yes. That's it."

"Dude!" Robbie protested. He held the ball under an arm. "You can't create life."

"Why not?" said Egberto. "Dr. Frankenstein did."

Robbie rolled his eyes. "You do know that Dr. Frankenstein wasn't real?"

But Egberto was unfazed.

He watched the movie *Frankenstein* for ideas and took lots of notes. He got his dad to drive him to Radio Shack for supplies. And he started searching for the perfect place to conduct his experiment.

Obviously, not the room he shared with his obnoxious little brother, Ruben. That kid got into everything, and Egberto didn't want his triumph spoiled by some sticky-fingered brat. Egberto's mom vetoed holding the experiment in a corner of the living room or the downstairs bathroom.

"The last thing we need is for someone to create new life in that bathroom," she said. "With two boys in the house, I can barely keep the funkiness under control."

★ ★ ★

When the solution came, Egberto was amazed he hadn't thought of it sooner. After all, it was the only place he could truly call his own, the only place that nobody ever snooped.

His desk at school.

Nobody would disturb his desk, not even his teacher, Mrs. Asante.

Perfect.

Now, the only challenge was how to set up the experiment. Egberto couldn't just haul in everything, spread it out in the aisle, and assemble it during class time. Mrs. Asante was easygoing, but not *that* easygoing.

The room got locked up shortly after school, so he couldn't do it then. Morning? Egberto was not a morning person — his brain didn't wake up until after first recess. So that left lunchtime.

★ ★ ★

One morning, three days before the fair, Egberto toted his box of supplies to school. He waited until silent reading time, then approached the teacher's desk.

"Can I stay in at lunch and work on my science fair project?" he asked Mrs. Asante.

She removed her red-framed glasses and rubbed her eyes. "It doesn't involve fire, does it?"

"No."

"Sharp knives, gunpowder, or dangerous chemicals?"

"Nope, nope, and nope," said Egberto. "I'm trying to create life, like Dr. Frankenstein."

"Oh." Mrs. Asante shrugged. "Okay, then. I'll be at a meeting in the teachers' lounge if you need any help."

And that was that.

Robbie volunteered to help Egberto. "After all," he said, "every Dr. Frankenstein needs an Igor."

They slowly ate their sack lunches while Mrs. Asante prepared for her meeting, waiting until every living being had left the room, except for the class hamster, Zorro. Then Egberto and Robbie got to work.

First, they emptied Egberto's desk. Then they lined the bottom with all the homework assignments that Egberto had refused to do. The creature needed a comfortable bed, after all. And maybe it would fuse with the assignments to create a kind of homework monster — that would be something to see!

In *Frankenstein*, the doctor had sewn together parts of

human bodies to make his monster. Egberto thought this was kind of gross. But worse, it wasn't practical, since no human, however small, could fit inside his desk.

After serious thought, Egberto had reached a better solution — one that wasn't quite so creepy. Still, when he opened the first jumbo freezer bag, he and Robbie had to take a step back.

"Eeeww!" said Robbie. "What the heck is that?"

"Roadkill," said Egberto. "It was in the freezer overnight, but I guess it's defrosting."

Covering his nose and mouth, Robbie said, "Pee-yew! What'll we do about the stink?"

After consideration, they borrowed the pine-scented air freshener spray from the restroom and unwrapped two packs of eucalyptus cough drops. The stink was tamed, but just barely.

Working quickly, Egberto stitched together the body of a cat, the head of a raccoon, and the tail of a squirrel — which had a tire mark across it, but still seemed serviceable. When the creature was finished, he and Robbie set up ten potato batteries around it.

"Will ten be enough?" asked Robbie.

"It better be," said Egberto. "We're out of spuds."

With copper wire, they linked the batteries to two electrodes on the creature's neck. Just before Egberto closed the desktop, Robbie added two items from his own desk: half of a peanut butter and jelly sandwich and some dried apricots.

"What's that for?" Egberto asked.

Robbie shrugged. "In case it comes to life and gets hungry."

"Good thinking."

The bell rang, and soon the rest of the class trickled into the room. By this time, Egberto and Robbie had cleaned up and taped the lid shut with masking tape.

When Mrs. Asante came in, she gave the desk a funny look. "What's going on here?"

"My science project," said Egberto. "It's, um, sensitive to light."

"Huh," said the teacher. "Smells like a forest."

The rest of the day passed smoothly. Just before the final bell, Egberto thought he heard a faint rustle from inside the desk. But when he lowered his head to listen, all was still. With a sigh, he chalked it up to general classroom noise.

Would his experiment really work? Maybe he'd bitten off more than he could chew.

On the walk home, Robbie buzzed with questions. "How long will it take? Will the thing follow your commands when it comes to life? Should we feed it cat food or raccoon food?"

To all questions, Egberto answered simply, "I don't know."

Sleep was a long time coming that night. Doubt alternated with excitement as he gazed out at the nearly full moon. If the creature came to life and he won the science fair, Egberto could rub Maya's face in it (his victory, not the creature). But if the experiment failed, he'd be a laughingstock.

It was a gamble. But then, he thought, great scientists accept great risks. If Egberto wanted to win, he had to take some chances.

★ ★ ★

The next morning, Egberto had planned to reach school early to check on his experiment. But after a sleepless night, he was running late.

As he and Robbie hustled through the stream of kids hurrying to their classrooms, Egberto found his way blocked by a tall girl with tightly woven braids. Maya Jackson. She stared down at him with bulging brown eyes.

"I hear you think you can beat me at the fair," Maya said.

Egberto played it cool. He raised one shoulder. "Everyone loses sometimes," he said.

"There's your mistake," she said.

"Oh?"

Maya gave him a pitying smile. "I'm not everyone. Prepare yourself for defeat." And with a little brushing-off gesture, she pushed past Egberto and headed down the hall.

His face felt hot. "Oh, yeah?" Egberto called after her. "We'll see about that!"

Robbie grimaced. "'We'll see about that'? That's the best you got?"

"She took me by surprise. I'm not afraid of Maya."

"Of course not," said Robbie. But he didn't sound as convinced as Egberto would've liked.

When they reached the classroom, Mrs. Asante and a bunch of kids were standing around Zorro the hamster's cage, looking serious. Robbie and Egberto joined them.

"What's up?" said Robbie.

Tiffany's voice wavered. "It's Zorro. He . . . he's dead."

"Dead?" asked Egberto. He inspected the cage. The exercise wheel, food bowl, and soup-can shelter stood there, same as always. But beside the wheel, a smear of blood stained the sawdust. "Where's his body?"

"That's a mystery," said Mrs. Asante.

"How'd it happen?" asked Robbie.

"That's a mystery, too," said Mrs. Asante. "The classroom door was locked overnight, but somehow a predator got inside. The custodian is investigating."

Egberto's gaze met Robbie's, and Egberto knew what they were both thinking. Robbie raised an eyebrow. *Could it be . . . ?*

Egberto frowned and shook his head. *No way.*

No way could his creature have come to life so soon. No way could it have escaped and gobbled up a hamster.

Could it?

Hurrying to his desk, Egberto squatted down and examined it. The masking tape strands still clung to the lid, but the lower ends hung free, like the desk wore a floppy straw hat.

Hmm . . .

Egberto lifted the lid a few inches and peeked. His hybrid creature still lay inside, surrounded by potato batteries. Egberto's shoulders relaxed. All was well.

But wait—the half sandwich and dried apricots had vanished! What was—

"Everything okay?" Mrs. Asante loomed over him.

Startled, Egberto let the lid drop and jumped to his feet. "Huh?"

"Your project," the teacher said. "Was it disturbed?"

"Oh, uh . . . no," said Egberto. "The tape just came unstuck." He smoothed the strands down. "See? All good."

Mrs. Asante called the class to order. But as Egberto sat down, he wondered. How good was it, really?

At lunch, Egberto and Robbie stayed in again. They added some pine-scented car fresheners to cover the smell. The wires had come loose from the electrodes. But Egberto didn't know if that was due to the creature moving or to his own sloppiness.

He reattached the wires and added four lemon batteries, just to be on the safe side. But his roadkill creation looked just as dead as ever.

Another night, another almost-full moon.

Overnight, nothing weird happened in their classroom, but by recess word had spread. All the class pets in the fourth-grade building—Waldo the rat, Beyoncé the garter snake, and a leopard gecko named Chuck—had disappeared. All that remained were blood smears.

Again, Egberto inspected his creature, but again it seemed motionless. The science fair was this afternoon—would his project work?

After school, Robbie helped him load the squirrel-cat-raccoon (squatcoon?) into a box and carry it to the multipurpose room where all the projects were being displayed. Most were the usual foam volcanoes, water cycle models, and so forth. But at one end of the room, a fancy curtained booth displayed the sign:

NUCLEAR FUSION REACTOR—MAYA JACKSON

Robbie winced. "Ooh, that's gonna be hard to beat."

"Don't worry," said Egberto. He bit his lip. "I've got this wired." He draped a black cloth over the box and set up his own sign, complete with dripping, monstery letters:

## THE CREATION OF LIFE—EGBERTO CRUZ

As a backup, he connected a car battery to the creature's electrodes. Just in case.

Later that afternoon, the multipurpose room teemed with parents and kids. Five judges strolled from exhibit to exhibit, watching demonstrations and taking notes. After the panel witnessed Robbie's Diet Coke Eruption display, Robbie came over to stand by Egberto.

"Good luck," he whispered.

Egberto wiped his sweaty palms on his pants and gave a tight nod.

The judges stood before him, two teachers, two parents, and one actual scientist. "Well, Egberto?" said the head judge. "Let's see what you've got."

Egberto cleared his throat. "From the earliest days, man has longed for the ultimate power—the power to create life. And now, at last . . . I have succeeded. Ladies and gentlemen, I give you"—he whisked the cloth away—"my creature!"

The five adults leaned over his box. Parents and kids looked on. The creature didn't twitch a whisker. Egberto's heart sank.

"Whew!" said the head judge. "This stinks."

"And it's not alive," the scientist said with a sneer. "Shall we go?" The group turned away.

Sneakily, Robbie bumped the box. "Wait, what was that?" he said.

"Your elbow," said the head judge. "Sorry, Egberto. Not this year."

Egberto clamped his lips together and nodded, not trusting his voice. He wasn't a scientist. He was just a kid who'd indulged in magical thinking. Really, what sane person would believe that a creature made of roadkill and homework could really come to life?

The judges moved off, headed for Maya's prizewinning project. Robbie patted his friend's shoulder. "Tough luck, dude."

Egberto nodded, staring up at one of the high windows. Real scientists don't cry, he reminded himself, even though he wasn't a real scientist. Absently, he noticed the full moon rise into view. It shone onto his table.

Robbie nudged him. "Come on. Let's go make fun of other people's projects."

Letting out a sigh, Egberto trudged after his friend. That was that. There would be no fourth-grade victory this science fair, no rubbing Maya's nose in it. No A in science.

He had failed.

Fellow fourth-graders shot him looks of sympathy.

Egberto and Robbie had almost reached Maya's station when the screams started. They turned.

Kids and parents pushed and shoved, trying to get away from a station down the row. Egberto's station.

"Run!" cried a teacher. "It's alive, it's alive!"

A quiver shot through Egberto's limbs. His heart hammered. Could it be . . . ?

An unearthly yowl filled the multipurpose room. Screams answered it. The crowd surged for the exits, carrying the boys along like twigs in a flood tide.

Egberto fought against the crowd. He jumped as high as he could, straining for a glimpse. What he saw chilled and thrilled him simultaneously.

Swollen to three times its size by the moon's magic, his squatcoon had reared up onto its hind legs. The creature howled and raked its claws at the mob, terrifying and triumphant.

And then the crowd swept Egberto onward.

Just before he was pulled out the door, Egberto happened to catch Maya Jackson's eye. She was scowling like someone had just sat on her birthday cake. He smiled at her.

Egberto turned to Robbie. "And that," he said as they spilled outside, "is how you win a science fair."

## WHAT REALLY HAPPENED

# GRRRRL POWER

t's okay for girls to play soccer, right? Or to have short hair? It's okay for girls to wear raggedy jeans, to run fast, to build tree forts in the woods, to shout loudly?

When I was a girl, back in the 1970s, one of the things that was a big deal was Women's Lib. It included a potential change to the US Constitution, the Equal Rights Amendment, which meant basically that women would be treated equally to men under the law. It didn't pass, but it did show that things were changing in our society. Earlier in our history, women were, for the most part, playing traditional roles—homemaker, mother, grandmother—and if they worked, it was in lower-paying jobs like secretary or housecleaner or preschool teacher.

So things were changing for women—and for girls, too. For everybody, really, and change is hard for a lot of people. A girl like me—a girl who wore holey jeans and soft, worn flannel shirts and had short hair and liked to play soccer—a girl like me was called a tomboy. What a stupid word, *tomboy*, as if an active girl isn't really a girl at all. Anyway, because I was a tomboy, I had run-ins with some people who thought girls should be ladylike and proper, "sugar and spice and everything nice."

My biggest enemy was the gym teacher at my school, Mr. Wasilenko. The boys called him "Waz." He was a former army sergeant, I think, a tough guy. He had brush-cut dark hair and lots of muscles; he wore buttoned-up polo shirts, black sneakers that squeaked on the shiny gym floor, and a whistle around his neck. And he did *not* think girls should be tomboys.

Now, I knew my way around a basketball court. I'd started playing soccer in the town league before there was a girl's team. I was the kickball queen at recess. But then there was gym class.

Back in those days, girls were supposed to wear bloomers when doing anything athletic. Not shorts! You probably don't even know what a bloomer is. Bloomers are like puffy skirt-shorts with elastic around the legs. So I was supposed to wear these horrible blue bloomers for gym. And while the boys played basketball, the girls were supposed to jump rope or sit on the benches at the side of the gym and watch the boys. It was really unfair.

I would like to tell you that this story has a happy ending. I wish I could say that I protested, that I went up to Mr. Waz and told him that I wanted to play basketball, too, and that he realized what a mistake he'd made, and let all the girls play basketball if they wanted to.

But I was just one skinny ten-year-old girl. I was a little scared of tough Mr. Waz.

So I never said anything. I kept quiet, like a good girl. And I never got to play basketball during gym class.

# FRANNY'S CHALLENGE

Along with every other junior high and senior high student in the school, I am sitting on the bleachers in the gym. That's almost three hundred people, plus all the teachers. We've been sitting here for an hour, and the gym has been getting hotter and stuffier, and everybody is getting more and more bored.

Mr. Bazinet, standing in the middle of the shiny basketball court with a clipboard, is running the show. Next to him stands my friend DaShae, who is reading her summer project report about volunteering for ten days at a soup kitchen in Chicago. Her voice is a monotone. Around me, students are whispering and slouching and generally not paying any attention.

I'm up next.

My best friend, Pip, sits beside me. "Are you nervous?" he whispers.

I nod. My butt is sore from sitting on the bleachers for so long, and I have a feeling like—you know when you have a balloon filled with helium and you let it go and it flies around the room squealing as all the air comes out?

Pip reaches over and takes my hand in his.

It keeps me from flying around the room squealing, at least.

Finally DaShae finishes reading her boring report and hands the microphone back to Mr. Bazinet. Rolling her eyes with relief, she finds her place again among the students in the bleachers.

Mr. Bazinet checks his clipboard. When he speaks, his voice booms out of the microphone. "And now for the last seventh-grade summer project report . . ." He flips a page. "Franny Prendergast presents the Girl Project."

Pip gives my hand a squeeze and lets me go.

I get to my feet and climb over him and a couple of other kids to get to the aisle, and then I go down to the basketball court. My sneakers squeak on the shiny floor as I cross to the center, where Mr. Bazinet hands me the microphone.

I look around. The bleachers are packed. Teachers are leaning against the walls. I see Pip, and a clump of football boys, and DaShae and my other friends, and then they blur together into one big, bored group that isn't going to listen to me.

My heart is pounding so hard it's almost making my whole body shake.

"The Girl Project," I say, and my voice, high and nervous-sounding, echoes in the gym. "This summer I learned ten things about being a girl, and I'm going to tell them to you now."

I take a deep breath.

I have my ten things, but they seem like a boring list with hard words like *gender stereotypes*, and *equality*, and *sexism*, and nobody's going to pay any attention. I shake my head.

Okay.

"Here is what I know," I say.

Girls are supposed to be skinny, I tell them. Girls are supposed to be curvy. Girls are supposed to wear makeup and nail polish and bikinis. Girls are supposed to like things that are pink and sparkly. Real girls are girly-girls. Every girl wants to date the quarterback of the football team. Girls are cheerleaders. But girls can grow up to be doctors or firefighters or plumbers or anything they want to be. The greatest athlete of all time, Babe Didrikson, was a girl.

"Don't be bossy," I tell them.

"Don't be loud." And my voice echoes off the gym walls.

"Be ladylike.

"Be quiet.

"Be a good girl.

"What a *mess*," I say.

*Mess . . . mess . . . mess* echoes in the gym.

"We have to do something about this," I tell the entire school, "because it's not fair."

Everybody, to my surprise, is paying attention. Sitting up, leaning forward. They may not be interested; they may just be waiting to see if I get in trouble. But they are *listening*.

"We can do the Girl Project all the time," I go on. "We can notice when things aren't fair, and we can do something about it."

I look into the crowd and catch Pip's eye. He is staring at me with laser intensity. He gives me a little nod that means, *Do it.*

Before, I wasn't sure I was going to do this, but now I am.

I think of something that once happened to the great athlete Babe Didrikson, who won Olympic medals for track and was an amazing basketball player and golfer. This boy named Red Reynolds, who was the star of the football team at her high school, challenged Babe to a boxing match. He told Babe to hit him as hard as she could, and he boasted, "You can't hurt me." He figured she wasn't tough enough.

Because she was a girl.

"I have a challenge," I tell everybody in the entire school. "Because there's something that's not fair right here in this gym, and we can do something about it."

"All right, that's enough," Mr. Bazinet interrupts, and reaches over to take the microphone from my hand. "You need to go sit down now."

I step away. "No," I say into the microphone. "It is my turn to talk. I am talking now, and you have to listen."

"Go get him, Franny!" shouts a voice from the crowd.

I feel a surge of strength. This is the basketball court. This is *my* place.

"We can do the Girl Project right now," I tell them.

I point to the huge painting of a blue-and-gold horse on one wall of the gym, over a basketball hoop. "Our team name is the Stallions," I say. I point to my own shirt. "The girls' teams are the Lady Stallions, right?"

"I assume you have a point, Miss Prendergast," Mr. Bazinet interrupts, and makes another grab for the microphone.

I step away from him again. "Lady Stallions," I repeat. "*Lady* Stallions? What does that even *mean*?"

A couple of people in the crowd laugh, and there are some mutters.

"A stallion is a boy horse. I mean, by definition it is," I say. "So how can you have a lady boy horse? It doesn't make any sense, does it?"

"No!" somebody shouts from the crowd, and a couple of other people join her. There's more muttering and shifting. They're not convinced, I can tell.

"So here's my challenge," I say, turning to face Mr. Bazinet, who is standing with his big arms folded, his face going red. "We change our team name to something more fair."

Mr. Baz shakes his head. He holds out his hand for the microphone, but I shake my head and keep my distance, because I know that once he has it, he won't give it back.

He speaks loudly so everybody in the gym can hear him. "Our team has been the Stallions for as long as we've had a school here. The name stays the same."

"The name stays the same," a boy shouts. The voice sounds like this kid on the football team named Kent.

"The name stays the same," a couple more people chant, and not just boys, either.

"Okay," I tell Mr. Bazinet. "Then I challenge you. I will shoot foul shots against any boy you choose, and if he wins, the name stays the same, and if I win, we get a new team name." I grip the microphone. He could so easily say no, and it'll be all over. "Deal?" I push.

I see Mr. Baz thinking it over. He narrows his eyes, looking me up and down, and I know what he sees—a twelve-year-old girl with short hair, wearing a skirt and basketball sneakers. I blink, trying to look harmless and sweet and . . . girly.

"The name stays the same," a group continues to chant, and I hear others telling them to shut up, and arguments and cheers.

Mr. Bazinet holds up a big hand, and slowly the gym falls silent.

I can see what he's thinking. He's going to put me in my place. I'm sure to lose, and that will show me. Slowly, he nods.

"Kent," he says with a nod toward the bleachers. "Get up here." He points at a teacher. "Get a ball."

★ ★ ★

The gym is silent. The air is hot and stuffy. Kent and I are at the foul line. He's a foot taller than I am and twice as heavy. He's wearing a Stallions football jersey and a ball cap covering his red hair, and slouchy jeans and sneakers. He's the center on the boys' varsity basketball team, and he's good.

I am good, too, but he might be better.

"The first to make five baskets wins," Mr. Bazinet's voice booms from behind us. He hands the basketball to Kent and then steps aside.

Kent turns and gives me a fake bow. "Ladies first," he says with a sneer, holding out the ball.

"No, thank you," I say sweetly. "You go ahead." I give him a big smile.

"Fine, since you're not a real lady, anyway," Kent says, and, shouldering me aside, he steps up to the foul line. "And," he adds, "you're going to lose."

He has a half grin on his face as he toes the line, bounces the ball once, and in a smooth, practiced move, takes his first foul shot.

*Swish.*

A bunch of people in the gym cheer loudly. Mr. Bazinet gives a smug-looking nod.

Kent retrieves the ball and passes it to me, throwing it just a little too hard. My hands sting as I catch it.

And I remember that Kent won a state tournament basketball game last year by making two foul shots in the last few seconds. He can handle the pressure. I'm not sure that I can.

My hands shaky, I start my foul-shot routine. Every basketball player has one. Carefully I line up my toes with the edge of the foul line. I bounce the ball three times without looking at the hoop, and bend my knees. I bounce again and look up at the hoop. Then a deep breath to settle myself, and I shoot.

My nervousness has made me tight, and as the ball leaves my fingertips it feels wrong.

The ball bounces on the rim and falls away.

*Miss.*

I hear Kent's triumphant shout, and some laughs from the crowd. One of the football players shouts, "Nice shot, Franny."

"One for Kent, zero for Franny," Mr. Bazinet says into the microphone.

Trying to shut out the noise, I fetch the ball and pass it to Kent.

He lines up, and, making it look easy, makes his second basket.

Smiling as if he's already won, he passes me the ball.

I do my routine, trying to stay loose, relaxed. I shoot.

*Swish.*

"Two for Kent, one for Franny," Mr. Baz says.

Then Kent lines up, does his one-bounce routine, and . . .

. . . he misses.

There's a loud groan from one section of the bleachers; a few people cheer or clap, almost all girls.

Kent shrugs and passes me the ball, and I step up to the line. I do my routine.

*Swish.*

Kent steps up to the foul line. He oh-so-carefully lines up his toes. He bounces the ball three times without looking at the hoop. Then he gives me a sly look and bends his knees.

It takes me a second, but then I see what Kent's doing. He's making fun of my foul-shot routine.

He bounces the ball again and looks at the hoop, and then he gives a little butt-waggle.

I *don't* do that.

He gives an exaggerated sigh — imitating my deep breath, I guess — and shoots the ball.

*Swish.*

Grrr.

But it's first one to make five baskets. It won't be long now.

And it's time to reveal the next part of my plan. Like Mr. Baz, I hold up my hand for silence. The crowd stills. "If I win, we're changing our team name to something more fair. I think this would be a good one." Carefully, I strip off my Lady Stallions T-shirt to reveal the shirt I'm wearing underneath.

Pip came up with the name, and he made the shirt. In big letters, the blue-and-gold T-shirt says Mighty Dragons, and there's a picture of a fire-breathing dragon in the center. There are some cheers, and some groans, and some clapping. Catching sight of Pip in the bleachers, I give him a grin, and he grins back.

I pick up the ball and do my routine, adding a little butt-waggle just for Kent, which makes a couple of people in the crowd laugh, and then I shoot.

The ball bounces on the rim and then drops through the net.

*Kent three, Franny three.*

The gym erupts in cheers. "You go, girl!" somebody shouts.

Kent steps up to the line. He's not half-smiling anymore; he looks mad. He does his one-bounce routine, he eyes the hoop, he shoots . . .

. . . and he misses.

Somebody in the crowd screams, and there's yelling and jeers.

"Settle down, settle down," booms Mr. Baz.

Kent passes me the ball. I line up to take my shot. I'm just about to shoot, when he gives a loud, fake sneeze, trying to distract me.

I hold on to the ball.

"Knock it off, Kent," comes a voice from the bleachers. I look over and can't believe it; it's a football player named Max, a good friend of Kent's. He's standing tall, and he nods at me and smiles.

Looking sullen, Kent scowls at the floor.

I do my routine again and make my basket.

"Kent three, Franny four," Mr. Bazinet says into the microphone.

Time for the last round.

The gym feels like it is full of crackling electricity. The kids are standing in the bleachers. "Kent, Kent, Kent," a few boys chant as Kent steps up to the line. His big hands take the ball; he bounces it once; he shoots.

*Swish.*

The crowd cheers, but their cheering grows even louder as I step up to the line.

With a scowl, Kent passes me the ball and then steps back. It's four to four. All I have to do is make this basket, and I win.

I bounce the ball three times, not looking at the hoop. I can feel sweat prickling on the back of my neck.

I bend my knees, and the crowd falls absolutely silent, waiting . . .

I bounce the ball again and look at the hoop.

The round, orange hoop, framed by the white backboard. The rest of the stuffy, crowded gym fades away.

I take a deep breath.

I shoot.

The ball leaves my hands and makes a smooth arc toward the basket.

As the ball soars through the air, I think of Babe Didrikson. When Babe was challenged to punch Red Reynolds, he thought she couldn't hit him because she was a girl. Well, Babe wound up and hit Ray so hard that she knocked him out.

The ball completes its arc.

*Swish.*

It goes through the hoop.

I win.

★ ★ ★

Everybody in the gym goes completely crazy, of course, whooping and stomping on the metal bleachers, and clapping and cheering.

Mr. Bazinet looks as if he's swallowed a frog.

A bunch of kids surge out of the stands to give me a high five or a hug, or pat me on the back — or on the top of my head — and Pip stands nearby, grinning his face off.

Holding the ball, Kent comes up to me with Max at his shoulder. "Good job, Franny," he admits.

I hold out my fist.

Max nudges him, and with his old half smile in place, Kent gives me a fistbump.

And then the final bell rings, and the Girl Project is over.

Or maybe it's not.

I know that I'm one person, and I can't change the world. But I can change a little piece of it. I can make a lot of noise when I see something that isn't fair. Maybe I'll be doing the Girl Project for my entire life.

Mike Winchell

# LUNCH AND RECESS

**Teachers giving you step-by-step** instructions, every minute of each class period planned out. Principals and hall monitors watching your every move in the hallway, controlled by policies and rules. These are all important parts of school, but sometimes they can make you feel like you don't have much freedom.

During lunch and recess, though, the way you spend your time is up to you. And as C. Alexander London, Vince and Nate Evans, and Varian Johnson show us, sometimes that's a good thing—and sometimes that's a bad thing.

# C. Alexander London

# A GIANT AMONG ANTS

When I was in fourth grade, I was a king among ants.

Literally.

There was this dirt patch next to the open blacktop where we had recess. There wasn't much of a playground, and I wasn't much of a player. Early in a brutal back-and-forth game of dodgeball one afternoon, I was eliminated (thankfully!) and took up my preferred place by the patch of dirt. On this particular day, my friend Eric and I found a piece of wood stuck in the dirt and we pried it out to see if it was anything worth playing with.

It wasn't.

But by pulling it out, we revealed a canyon filled with ant holes and anthills swarming with big black ants. We'd uncovered an entire subterranean ant city! For days after the discovery, we would stand around this canyon and watch the ants bustling to and fro.

I made up stories about the ants and spent my free time (and a lot of class time) creating a newspaper based on the imagined happenings in the ant city. There was a mayor and a general who I placed in a heated public feud over expanding the colony, and there was a weekly column written by the ant queen. There was also an ever-present fear of the "Red Menace"—a term I believed I'd invented to describe the violent red ants that lived under the tree on the other side of the blacktop.

Soon, I grew bored with merely watching and imagining. I wanted to get involved in the life of my ant city. I placed a twig in a mound of dirt just above the canyon and called it a temple. I plucked a caterpillar from a tree and smashed its head with a pebble, letting its green gooey guts spill out. Then I impaled the unfortunate creature as a gift to the citizens, who ascended from the canyon to eat the generous meal I'd given them. One caterpillar could feed a hundred of these ants.

I wondered what the ants imagined about me, the giver of violent gifts from above.

My stories drew the attention of other kids. They gathered around to watch my caterpillar sacrifices, to celebrate the swarms of ant citizens that had come to feed, and the kids wanted their own chance to smash a caterpillar.

My rule was absolute, however, and I didn't want to confuse my ant subjects: Only *I* could smash the caterpillars for my ants.

A boy named Agedi soon decided he'd had enough of my rule over the ant colony, and he started a second civilization with the red ants under the tree across the blacktop. He made up his own stories, sacrificed his own caterpillars, and ruled the red ants as I ruled the black ants. The busy blacktop sat like an ocean between us.

But history shows that oceans demand to be crossed.

Soon, my sacrifices moved from the temple. I would place a caterpillar to the left of the little twig, and the ants would devour it. Then another farther to the left, and they would go to that. I lured them farther and farther from their canyon every day. I lured them across the blacktop one caterpillar at a time. They'd gotten so used to the easy food, it seemed like most didn't hesitate to follow in a long ant column. I lured them straight to the home of the red ants.

Not all survived the journey. It was recess, and many were stomped and crushed beneath the uncaring sneakers of boys at play. But for those ants who survived the journey all the way across the blacktop, I was sure glory would be theirs.

"WAR BREAKS OUT! INVASION OF THE REDS BEGINS!" read the headline on the newspaper I drew in my notebook during social studies that day. I couldn't wait for recess to see what had happened now that I'd led my ants to war. Agedi was curious, too, and we raced outside to witness the battle.

It was over when we got there. A few black ants remained, but they were scattered all around the roots of the tree, and for every single one of them, there were a dozen red ants. The red ants had swarmed and destroyed the black ants without mercy. I saw columns of tiny red ants carrying my black ones away on their backs, vanishing into their holes in a straight line, grim victory marches after a war well won.

I ran across the blacktop, dodging balls better than I ever did when I was actually playing dodgeball, and I found that my canyon was now empty. One or two stray black ants skittered around the temple twig, and another two or three wandered in the ruins of their colony, but the spark of life was gone.

Across the blacktop Agedi and his friends had moved on, but I stood a minute longer over my once mighty city, and it broke my heart. I knew I was responsible for its destruction, but I didn't know exactly why. I'd led my ants to slaughter and I hadn't even witnessed the battle. There'd be no point in even drawing a newspaper after recess, because what ant was left to read it? (As if the ants had ever read it at all.)

Soon, Eric stood beside me.

"The ants are gone?" he asked.

"Uh-huh," I told him.

"Oh, well ... *tag!*" he yelled, slapping my shoulder. "You're it!"

And then he ran, and I didn't hesitate to run after him.

I was "it" and had "it" responsibilities to attend to.

I wasn't king of the ants anymore and never would be again.

# C. Alexander London

# ANTPOCALYPSE NOW

Antonio followed the Drone in front of him like he always followed the Drone in front of him. The Drone behind Antonio followed him the same way. They carried crumbs on their backs like they always carried crumbs on their backs.

For an ant with Antonio's job, it was a day like any other.

Until one of the News Ants stood in his way, right in the center of the tunnel, and cried out a headline as loud as he could.

"Feast from the Skies! Food for all! The Great Giant has given us another gift!"

The ant in front of Antonio stopped short, so that Antonio smacked into his back, and they both dropped their crumbs.

"Sorry about that," Antonio said.

"Oh don't worry one bit!" the ant in front of him said, his antennae bouncing cheerily atop his head. "Who needs to carry crumbs when the Great Giant above gives us caterpillars? It's a sugar-sweet day, my friend!"

Antonio didn't like how the other ants called him friend

when they didn't even know his name. That was something about the ant colony that had made Antonio uncomfortable for as long as he could remember. Everyone assumed that he was just like them, that he thought the same way and talked the same way, and was content to do the same as everyone else did no matter what.

But Antonio felt different.

He wasn't like the other ants in his colony, and he didn't want to be. He wanted to be more than just a Drone, destined to carry food on his back his whole life, as if that was all he'd been born for. He didn't feel bad about feeling different. He *wanted* to be different. He *liked* being different.

And that was the danger.

For a colony ant, being different was dangerous. Every ant was supposed to be the same and want the same things and like the same things.

And all the ants liked the caterpillars that the Great Giant kept leaving for them to feast upon.

Antonio didn't think the Great Giant who brought the caterpillars was to be trusted. He had seen so many ants trapped under the feet of giants that he had to wonder: What made this one Great Giant want to feed the ants rather than crush them? Was the Great Giant different from all the other giants, merciful and generous to those much smaller than he?

Antonio doubted it. His own uncle had been crushed beneath a giant's feet two seasons ago, and ever since, he didn't trust any giant as far as he could throw him. And although he could carry one thousand times his body weight over his head like every other ant, he could not throw a giant. Not at all.

"Let's go to the temple!" the other ant cheered and raced off for the surface above the colony. The ants behind Antonio also wanted to get to the surface where the caterpillar had appeared, impaled on a stick, and they charged forward. Antonio was swept up in the great surge, carried into the sunlight by the sheer excitement of his fellow ants. It wasn't until they'd burst from underground and stood at the edge of their great canyon that he could step aside and let the others rush to where the caterpillar lay.

The caterpillar was a plump green beast, taller than three ants standing atop one another and longer than a dozen standing end to end. Its hairy back lay flat against the dirt with its belly pointed to the sky. Its head had been smashed so that the pale green goo of its guts leaked out. From that goo, the ants feasted. Some simply shoved their jaws full of the stuff, while others tore off chunks of the monster's belly to carry on their backs into the colony, where babies in the nursery cried to be fed. Somewhere in the tunnels, the Queen herself sat upon her throne and waited for the choicest cuts of caterpillar to be brought by her Royal Tasters.

This caterpillar was several lengths away from the usual spot at the temple stick. Although none of the other ants seemed concerned, Antonio kept his distance, unsure what it meant that the giant had brought this caterpillar but had not put it near the temple.

"Hey!" someone shouted. "There's another one!"

All antennae shifted, and indeed, several more lengths away, another caterpillar had been given to the ants, just like the first, with its head bashed in and green goo spilling out. It lay on its side, just at the edge of the great desert, where the giants' shoes stomped and the heat shimmered up from the endless expanse of smooth black stone.

"A feast day for the ages!" the ants cheered, and a new line raced to feed on the second caterpillar. Some of the ants caught the scent of a third, out on the black stone itself, and a line had begun to zig and zag toward it. There were no giants around — they'd all gone inside to their great brick castle, where bells rang all day long.

"Hey, Antonio, what's wrong? Not hungry?" His best friend, Antioch, stood beside him, chewing on a juicy piece of caterpillar. "It's good," he added, taking another bite. Pale green juice dribbled down his chin.

Antonio shrugged.

Antioch chewed loudly and spoke with his mouth full. "The giant who brings this food is super nice," he said. "Look how much he brought today!"

A fourth caterpillar had been discovered, even farther across the blacktop, and more ants were pouring from the canyon to devour it. At this rate, every ant in the whole colony would be out on the blacktop, feasting.

Antonio feared the giant's gruesome gifts.

"I don't trust the giant," Antonio told his friend.

Antioch dropped the plump green blob of guts, and his sharp jaws hung slack and open in shock.

"Shhh!" he scolded. "How can you say such thing?" He looked over his shoulder. "Don't trust? No . . . you mustn't say you don't trust!"

Antonio shook his head. "I don't think *you* should trust the giant, either. Look how far from home he's leading everyone."

Antioch glanced up and saw that the line of ants stretched to a sixth and then a seventh caterpillar, over halfway across the blacktop.

Even the Queen herself had come out, carried on her royal travel throne by her entourage of Royal Travel Throne Carriers.

Antioch looked back at Antonio and shook his head. "It's not about trusting the giant," Antioch warned him. "It's about *you*. It's about the colony. You can't say you don't trust the giant. *Everyone* trusts the giant."

"But I'm different," said Antonio.

"But your mistrust doesn't hurt the giant, Antonio . . . it hurts *us*. It hurts all antkind."

"That's nonsense."

"No it isn't," Antioch protested. "All of ant society relies on trust. Marching in a line takes trust that the ant in front of you knows where he's going and that the ant behind you is following. Digging tunnels in the dirt takes trust that other ants are also digging so that the tunnels meet. All these tiny acts of trust from one ant to another add up to create our civilization. That's all civilization is, anyway. Just tiny acts of trust from one ant to another over and over and over. Millions of acts of trust. So you saying you don't trust the giant is like saying you don't trust all the other ants who *do* trust the giant. Once ants stop trusting, well, it'll all fall apart."

Antonio shook his head. "We don't have to think the same way to get along," he said.

"We *do*," said Antioch. "And I'm going to get some more caterpillar, just like everyone else. I hope you'll join me."

Antioch turned to go, but Antonio didn't follow.

"Suit yourself," said Antioch sadly. "Though I guess you always do."

When Antioch had crossed the blacktop and disappeared into the swarm of other ants, Antonio turned and went back into the tunnels to wait for the strange feast day to end.

He ground his jaws together; he grumbled to himself. His friend had no right to criticize him for being different. So what if he was different? The world wasn't going to fall apart just because ants disagreed with each other once in a while, was it?

He heard shouting from above, almost as if the heavens were answering his unspoken question. There were cries and screams, too. His antennae prickled in the air. He sensed the vibrations of his colony, smelled the scent of their great feasting line, but he smelled another smell, too — the smell of blood. Ant blood.

Lots of it.

He raced back toward the surface, running through empty tunnels, turning this way and that, until he popped back into the sunlight and caught another smell with his antennae, a third, powerful smell that he had never smelled before yet knew immediately from instinct: Red Ants.

Elders of Antonio's colony told the young ones nightmare stories about Red Ants:

*If you don't clean your tunnel, the Red Ants will carry you off while you sleep!*

*If you don't bow to the Queen, the Red Ants will steal your food while you sleep!*

*If you don't carry your load, the Red Ants will eat your head while you sleep!*

Red Ants were smaller than Black Ants, but they were supposed to be stronger, and their jaws were sharper, their bites more ferocious, and their colonies warlike and terrible.

Antonio had always thought Red Ants were just stories used to scare children into behaving, but he knew now they were real. The Red Ants had come.

When he reached the edge of the great expanse of blacktop, he saw a sight for which his sense of smell could never have prepared him: A Red Ant colony pouring from the ground on the opposite side of the blacktop had met his Black Ant colony in battle beneath the scorching sun.

A few News Ants remained close to the edge of the blacktop, and one of them cried out what Antonio had feared: "WAR BREAKS OUT! INVASION OF THE REDS BEGINS!"

Then the News Ants raced off to join the battle, and Antonio was left alone again to watch.

Ant tore at ant, jaw clashed with jaw. The crunch of breaking armor echoed across the air. The ant that Antonio had run into that morning was running in circles, the legs from one side of his body torn off, carried away by three small Red Ants who held the unfortunate's limbs out in front of themselves like clubs, smacking and swinging the terrible weapons to clear their path.

It was the most horrible sight Antonio had ever seen.

And then he remembered his friend, Antioch, somewhere in the fray.

Antonio hesitated, but then ran into the battle, weaving around the bodies of the fallen.

"Antioch!" he cried out. "Antioch!"

A Red Ant charged at him, but Antonio dodged the first snap of the smaller ant's jaws, and then kicked him in the side so that he rolled onto his back. He moved to bite the weak place between links in the Red Ant's shell, but the ant cried out, a word in his own language that Antonio didn't recognize. He could smell the Red Ant's terror and see the quiver of his antennae. He had no quarrel with this ant. Why should he kill him?

Antonio raced on, leaving the Red Ant alive.

"Antonio?"

He heard a faint voice, the voice of his friend, Antioch. Antonio ran to Antioch where he lay. One leg was missing, one antenna was bent, and his shell was cracked clean across his forehead. His voice was faint.

"I'm here!" Antonio wrapped his friend in his front legs, hugging him.

"I thought you . . ." Antioch struggled to speak. "I thought you wouldn't come. You said we were fools to trust the giant."

"You were," said Antonio. "I'm not out here to scold you. I'm out here to *help* you. My friend."

"I'm sorry I didn't listen," Antioch said.

"There's nothing to be sorry for," said Antonio. "You did what you did for good reasons, just like I did. One of us doesn't have to be wrong for the other to be right."

"But the colony . . . ," Antioch said.

Antonio looked around the battlefield. Black Ants were falling to the right and left, and more Red Ants were charging from their side of the blacktop, outnumbering the Black Ants by as many as a hundred to one. He saw the Queen and her Royal Travel Throne Carriers swarmed so heavily by Red Ants that there was no hope of saving any of them.

Then he heard a bell, a bell from the building of the giants. And the doors opened.

"The colony is lost," Antonio said. "And if we don't go, we'll be lost, too, crushed beneath the giants' shoes."

"I can't walk," said Antioch. "Leave me."

"No," said Antonio. "I can carry you."

He hoisted Antioch onto his back with ease. His friend groaned with the pain of being lifted, but he allowed himself to be carried. Antonio ran with his friend, away from the battle, away from the Red Ants, who had ceased attacking when the giants began to reach the blacktop.

Soon, a new set of cries rang out as ants, both Red and Black, found themselves trampled under the feet of giants. The Red Ant Antonio had spared was not spared by a giant's careless shoe. Such was the way of war. Good or ill, friend or enemy, heroic or brave: All could be smashed beneath a giant's foot in an instant.

Antonio looked away from the horrible scene. He did not wish to see such destruction ever again. He ran with Antioch to the canyon they had called home, but then kept running, into the grass beyond the dirt, where he would dig new tunnels and nurse his friend back to health. Maybe, one day, if they stuck together, they would find a new colony, a place where an ant could be himself, unique. If they couldn't find such a colony, perhaps they would start one themselves, for it wasn't a Queen who made a colony, but two Drones deciding to trust each other, no matter what, even if they didn't always agree. Even if they were different.

When they reached the grass, Antioch noticed something strange from his spot on Antonio's back. "I think," he said, "one of the giants just waved to us."

"That's just the pain talking," Antonio told him.

"I don't know," said Antioch. "This giant made me think of you. He looked . . . *different*."

"No," snapped Antonio, unable to contain his anger. "The giants are all the same."

Antioch's silence spoke his disagreement loudly.

"Do you trust me?" Antonio asked Antioch, looking for reassurance.

"I trust you," said Antioch.

Antonio smiled, and with that, they entered an unfamiliar tunnel and left the world they knew, the colony they'd lost, and the land of caterpillars and giants far behind.

# Vince Evans

# THE TEST

Not many kids can pee in school and become more menacing. I'm not talking about a nervous kid who gets asked a tough question by the teacher and wets himself. This wasn't just some toddler in kindergarten, either...

It was fifth grade, and Tony was one of the largest kids in the class. He had been arguing with the teacher off and on for a few hours, like some knuckleheads do when they're bored and just want to leave class. After the last outburst, Tony asked if he could go to the bathroom. The request was denied. Tony pushed back in his chair. Remaining seated, he unzipped and began urinating, directing the stream at anyone who looked his way. All kids like to see the teacher's authority challenged. But this was different. This was a glimpse of a world without rules. This was anarchy.

The teacher remained unaware until there was a good-size pool of urine on the floor, and then he angrily ordered Tony to the principal's office. Tony left, reminding the teacher with a smile, "I said I had to go to the bathroom." There were no funny nicknames afterward, no "Tony Tinkles" or "Puddles," just total terror.

I'm sorry if that grossed you out, but it's important to tell the truth here. That's what I was up against: Tony the Terror.

Tony and I had had a few run-ins in the past, including the time he was recruited to beat me up by the only two kids in our grade who were smaller than me. My older brother bailed me out of that jam by acting as my bodyguard, but he'd since graduated to another school. This time I was on my own. The situation was simple enough the way Tony explained it to me that morning. Tony and I had the same afternoon math class, and I had a reputation for being an egghead.

"I'm going to copy off your test today," Tony said. "Just make sure you hold it up so I can see it."

That was it, short and to the point. Then Tony walked away. I don't remember if there was a verbal threat, but I do know it was implied. I was doomed. I mean, if I didn't know it before, I sure knew it after witnessing the Urination Incident: Tony didn't bluff. His threats were promises. And like all good threats, this one was delivered early, with the moment of reckoning not for hours, giving me plenty of time to agonize. I was terrified of the beating, but there was an even worse concern: If I allowed this, if he copied from me today, where would it stop? Would Tony copy all my tests from now on? Would I have to start doing his homework, too? On top of that misery, I'd be a marked man, a target for any of the other academically challenged bullies. I *had* to think of a way out.

Like most kids in a bad situation, I did nothing all day. No plans, no recruiting of friends or talking to teachers. I just fantasized about events that would save me: a fire, the teacher suddenly getting sick, a dinosaur crushing the school.

All that daydreaming took me right up to math class, where X+Y was about to equal a fist in my face. I slumped into my seat. Tony had positioned himself in the desk directly behind me (not a good location if he started urinating again). The tests were passed around and I slowly started answering the questions, still sort of lost in a daydream-like nightmare . . . was the dinosaur ever going to crush the school? Maybe Tony forgot? A quick kick to the back of my chair informed me that he hadn't. There was a second kick and a whisper that I couldn't really hear, but I'm sure it wasn't "Good luck." I curled my test upward and leaned to the side to give Tony a clear view. This was bad. I was doing exactly what I didn't want to do.

Then an idea crept into my brain. Maybe I could stall, pretend like the questions were too tough. Tony would give up on me for fear of not finishing his own test. I launched into what I'm sure was some terrible acting: I scratched my head, counted on my fingers, put in answers only to slap the table and erase them. Tony reviewed my performance with three swift kicks to my chair. Those kicks finally knocked my brain into high gear. It was simple, really. And I was desperate enough to try anything. I would take a dive, throw the test, and flunk it. I had good grades; my average could handle one bad test. If I proved I was a math moron, then I'd be free!

Now I answered the questions quickly and held the paper up high. *Take a look at this, sucker,* I thought. Fear of Tony kept me cautious, though. Some of these questions were easy. He'd know the answers were wrong. So I mixed some right ones in with the wrong.

It wasn't a long test, and the teacher rapidly graded them and returned them as the bell rang. I don't remember my grade. I know it wasn't a complete F—I did answer some questions right. But it wasn't passing. I did one last bit of encore acting: I gasped and clutched my chest upon seeing my score. I never looked back. I didn't try to slip away, either. I just trudged slowly toward the door, mixed in with the mass of kids.

Suddenly Tony was in front of me, blocking my way. Glaring, he held the crumpled test in his clenched fist inches from my nose. I stood there motionless. He leaned forward and, with utter disgust, grumbled, "I thought you were smart."

That was it. He turned and walked away. It was as if I'd betrayed some great friendship. I'd let him down. For him there was an order to things: He threatens me and I give him what he wants. I'd twisted that. In some small way I may have shown him a terrifying world without rules. Now he was the one on the other side of anarchy.

I managed to steer clear of Tony after that, but it didn't take much effort. He never sought me out. Sometimes he was even friendly to me. I assumed it was because I'd proven I was no egghead. I was just another kid failing school.

# Nate Evans

# THE BIG BULLY BACKFIRE

et me say this right up front: I'm a nice guy. I've volunteered at an animal shelter (picking up poop, no less). I give to a charity that assists kids who live in poverty. I even help old ladies cross the street. But even nice guys can be jerks once in a while, and back in sixth grade, I was—I hate to admit this—a jerk.

It started one day during recess. My elementary school used to pass out balls for us to play with, and my friends and I wanted to shoot some hoops. A little kid, probably a third-grader, wanted the same basketball that I did. I wrestled him for it, yanked it away, and then called him a punk. Something like that. My friends and I messed around on the basketball court until the bell rang, and I didn't think much about it again . . . except for a marble-size ball of guilt that was rolling around in my stomach somewhere.

That afternoon I walked home from school, and there was the kid from recess waiting for me . . . with his big brother. *Oh, crud!* I thought. I didn't know this kid lived in my apartment complex. And I sure didn't know that he had a big brother.

"That's him," said the kid, pointing at me. The big brother growled, pulled a pair of pliers from his pocket, and stomped toward me like the Terminator. I wasn't sure what he was planning to do with those pliers, but I didn't stick around to find out. I scrambled for home like a yipping dog.

Now, it just so happened that my stepbrother was also home. I thought about telling Bob, my seventeen-year-old stepbrother who drove a cool motorcycle, what happened, and getting him to go teach that bully with the pliers a thing or two . . . but I didn't. That marble-size ball of guilt rolling around in my gut was now the size of a grapefruit, and I knew that I was responsible for what had happened. I'd acted like a jerk to a little kid, and he was getting revenge. I couldn't help feeling like I deserved it. My crummy action during recess caused a reaction, just like a physics experiment. I had no one to blame but myself. Feeling miserable, I climbed into bed at 4:15 with nothing but my sour guilt for an afternoon snack.

The next day after school, the brothers were waiting for me again. The goon I knew as "Pliers" snarled like a pit bull and then started spitting names at me—unimaginative stuff like "Four Eyes" (because I wore glasses), but it still stung. I skulked away, fear and guilt boiling in my stomach.

This kept happening for the next few days. Sometimes the bully brothers were waiting for me and sometimes they weren't, but I lived in an enveloping, acidic fog of anxiety. I still wasn't talking to anyone about what was happening.

Then one afternoon, my friend Gary walked home with me. I wanted to show him some new superhero comic books I'd bought recently. We were talking about Batman and the X-Men and dynamic comic artists like Jack Kirby, and I was so caught up in our discussion that I forgot about the whole bully situation. Gary was tall and tough, and he was also awesomely talented— he starred as the Artful Dodger in our class production of *Oliver*. (When Gary grew up, he got even taller and tougher and joined the military. I'm proud to still call him my friend.) I can't quite remember how it played out exactly, but Gary stopped to tie his shoe or something and it must have appeared as if I was walking home from school by myself, as usual. That was when the evil goon, Pliers, jumped out from behind the nearest building shouting, "Where ya goin', Four Eyes?!"

Like one of the superheroes we'd just been talking about, Gary stepped up beside me, bristling with anger and tons of attitude, and roared, "Don't call my friend 'Four Eyes'!"

I'll never forget what happened next: Pliers went white as notebook paper. His mouth hung open; his eyes bulged in fear. Pliers suddenly looked like a puny villain who'd been stunned by the mighty fist of Superman. He'd gotten a huge helping of "Truth, Justice, and the American Way" courtesy of Gary, the sixth-grade Superman, and you could tell Pliers was choking on it.

With a strangled yelp, Pliers ducked back behind the building and he was gone. Just like that. Like a magic trick.

"Who was that dude?" Gary asked.

"No one," I replied. And it was true. I never saw Pliers again. I was genuinely surprised to discover that he was a cowardly cream puff. Sure, he could be brave when facing off against a skinny kid like me. But when confronted with a real challenge, like Gary the Super Sixth-Grader, Pliers collapsed like a skyscraper sculpted from snot. But I couldn't gloat. Hadn't I done the same kind of stupid bully moves when I'd grabbed the basketball from that poor third-grade kid?

I realized that I'd earned some awful consequences with my actions that day. But Pliers had, too. He'd made picking on me a hobby. That was his choice. We'd both been jerks. We'd both made stupid choices. And justice was served when we were both knocked down by the big bully backfire.

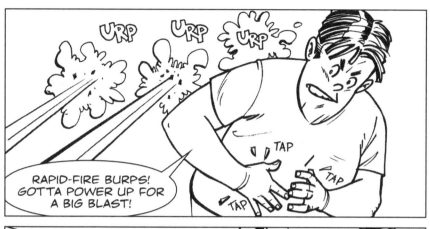

# Varian Johnson

# OUT OF MY TWIN'S SHADOW

There are a lot of great things about growing up as an identical twin. If you ever run out of clean clothes, a fresh shirt and pair of jeans are only a closet away. You always have someone available whenever you want to play *Combat* on your state-of-the-art Atari 2600 video game console. And you always have someone to talk to, about anything and everything.

Then there's the bad—like when you and your twin are so close, you don't quite know how to function when he's not around.

That's exactly what happened to me when I started seventh grade at Williams Middle School. For the first time, my brother and I were in different classes, something that I didn't even consider as a possibility until I received my schedule. One of those classes was during the school's lunch period, and it turned out that my brother ended up in first lunch and I had second. And of course, the few friends we had from elementary school were scheduled for first lunch, as well.

I remember agonizing over how lunch was supposed to work. Not just the part where I had to find new people to sit with—I didn't even know *when* I was supposed to go to the cafeteria. Was I supposed to line up with my fourth period class, and we'd head to the cafeteria together like in elementary school? Was I supposed to go to my fifth period class first, drop off my books, then go to lunch? I was a good kid; I prided myself on knowing, understanding, and following the rules. The last thing I wanted was to get in trouble, especially on my first day of school. I finally summoned the courage to ask my homeroom teacher about lunch . . . and she responded by basically calling me an idiot.

I struggled during my entire seventh-grade year. I never felt comfortable talking to other students, and I got swindled for money and food more times than I'd like to admit. When my brother and I ended up with the same schedule in eighth grade, I fell back into the familiar routine of deferring to him for almost everything.

Things ultimately changed for me in ninth grade. My high school's incoming freshman class was huge, and most students had requested to take gym class instead of Air Force Junior Reserve Officer Training Corps (JROTC). After asking parents and students to reconsider, the school eventually resorted to randomly selecting students to take JROTC. Of course, I was picked.

It turned out that JROTC was exactly what I needed. I excelled at the history lessons inside the classroom and the drill instructions in the parking lot behind the school. I loved wearing a uniform—it was the one day of the week when there was no mistaking me for my brother.

And I had a very gifted teacher, Sgt. Leonard Fields, who saw something in me that I didn't even see in myself. I wasn't just a smart kid. I wasn't just a boy that could follow rules. I could be a leader. I *was* a leader. And I don't know if I would have ever learned that if I hadn't been forced outside of my brother's shadow.

# Varian Johnson

## THE STORY

# SPEAKING UP

While Dad talked to Francine, her head nodding at whatever first-day-of-middle-school advice he was doling out, I sat in the backseat and reviewed my schedule. I didn't know why — in the three weeks since orientation, I'd memorized the time and location of each class. I'd even found the school layout online and had mapped my path from room to room. I still didn't understand when I was supposed to go to lunch, but Francine and I had already decided to ask a teacher about it.

I folded my schedule and crammed it into my backpack. Dad had joined the long line of cars snaking into the parking lot. We lived within walking distance of school, but Dad really wanted to drop us off on the first day.

Or if I'm being honest, *I* wanted Dad to.

As we inched forward, kids streamed by — some walking, some riding bikes and skateboards. Ahead of us, a kid exited his car and ran off to join a few boys passing by. He didn't even look back as his mother pulled out of the line.

Dad sighed. "What do you think, guys? Want me to let you off here?"

"Sure," Francine said, already unfastening her seat belt.

"Maureen?" He looked at me in the rearview mirror.

I shrugged, which was about the best I could offer.

He turned to my sister. "Stay in. I'll drop you off in the front."

"But, Dad —"

"Be patient, Francine." He tugged the ponytail protruding from her gray knit cap. "It won't kill you to wait."

After a few minutes, we reached the front of the line. "Try to have fun," Dad said as we exited the car. "Think of it as an adventure."

I followed Francine into the sea of students, pretty much placing my feet where hers had just been. We waved to a few of the kids we knew, but kept moving toward the gym. That was where we'd agreed to meet Nikki and Tasha. Most of our other friends were attending a different middle school.

"You sure you're okay?" Francine asked. "You haven't said much all morning."

"I never say anything." I wanted to remind her that talking was her job and thinking was mine — at least, that was what Mom and Dad always used to say. But there was no point in telling her what she was already supposed to know.

"It'll be okay," she said. "Most of our classes are together."

"Four out of seven isn't exactly an overwhelming majority."

Francine smiled at me as she readjusted her knit cap. It was too big, but that hadn't stopped her from buying it. With her cap, old-school hip-hop T-shirt (she didn't even know who Run-D.M.C. was until she googled them), and scuffed-up Converses, she seemed determined to make sure no one confused us for each other today.

Which, quite frankly, wasn't going to happen.

Francine and I were identical twins. Even though we looked nothing alike, in my opinion — Francine was a quarter of an inch taller, I had a small scar on my chin from when I fell in the bathtub, and there were like a thousand other differences — all most people seemed to focus on were the similarities. Our eyes. Our mouths. The way our heads tilted when we were thinking, and the way our shoulders bobbed when we laughed. It had taken six years to get the kids and teachers at O'Conner Elementary to see us as different. Now we were starting all over again.

I slowed down as we neared the gym. Nikki and Tasha were waiting for us, like they said they would be. And they were wearing knit caps.

"You three dressed alike?" I asked.

Francine turned toward the girls. She sighed — or maybe even growled — then plowed forward. I had to hurry to keep up.

"Why are you guys wearing those?" Francine asked. "When you asked what I was wearing, I didn't think you were going to copy me!"

"I was having a bad hair day," Tasha said. "And when I texted Nikki this morning, she said she wanted to wear one, as well."

"What's the big deal?" Nikki added. "It's not like you're the only person that can wear a knit cap to school." She turned to me.

"I've got an extra if you want to wear one, too."

I shook my head. From the way Francine was glaring at them, I could tell that was the right answer.

The bell rang, and we shuffled into the building. It was hard not to feel boxed in, being surrounded by so many students. The hallways at O'Conner had never been nearly as crowded.

Unlike all those cheesy teen TV shows, we went to our first period class before homeroom. It was life science, a class that Francine and I had together, and thankfully she didn't argue when I picked the seat behind her. But when Mr. Diggs took roll and said, "Francine Carter," she raised her hand and shook her head.

"Please call me Fran."

My eyes bored a hole into the back of her head. Since when was she *Fran*?

"Fran it is," he replied. "And should I call you Maur?" he asked me.

He laughed. No one else did.

"Maureen is just fine," I said.

After roll, he spent the next forty-five minutes talking about the beauty of the circle of life. Not the most interesting topic, but at least it kept my mind occupied.

Then came homeroom.

Mrs. Barbosa went over a few school rules (which I'd already learned from my orientation packet), then she let us read until the bell rang. I tried to catch Francine's attention (and no, I was not about to start calling her Fran) in order to get her to ask the teacher a question about lunch, but she was too busy reading *Pride and Prejudice* to look my way. It was the latest of the big, old, boring books she'd picked up this summer. She'd tried to get me to read it, but there was no way I was reading something like that over my summer break—not when I had Dad's entire comic book collection to go through.

Anyway, Francine never looked my way, so finally I raised my hand to ask the teacher myself.

"Yes, Fran?" Mrs. Barbosa said.

I didn't bother correcting her. "I'm a little confused about when I'm supposed to go to lunch."

She motioned for me to approach the front. A few seats ahead of me, Scott Casey read a graphic novel at his desk. I didn't really know him—he had gone to elementary school with us, but was always in a different class. He was also one of the smartest kids in our grade.

I slowed down and tried to see what he was reading. He must have sensed me looking at him, because he hunched over and covered the book.

Mrs. Barbosa snapped her fingers. "I don't have all day."

I sped up, almost tripping over Scott's backpack, then handed her my schedule. "You're supposed to go between fourth and fifth period," she said.

"Yes," I began. "But does that mean that I'm supposed to go to class first? Or am I supposed to go to the cafeteria, and then go to class?"

"What are you talking about? Of course you're supposed to go to class."

"Okay, so I go to fifth period first, and then we go to the cafeteria."

"Didn't you hear me — you have lunch between fourth and fifth periods." She narrowed her eyes at me. "Are you trying to be smart?"

"No, ma'am," I mumbled. "I just . . . never mind. I understand," I lied.

After the bell rang, and before Francine walked off to her next class without me, I grabbed her. "Why didn't you ask the teacher about the lunch schedule?"

"I figured I'd follow everyone else," she said. "It's just lunch. How hard can it be?"

Pretty hard, it turned out.

Apparently, I was supposed to go to lunch straight after fourth period, not go to fifth. (Unlike in elementary school, we didn't all line up and go to the cafeteria together.) So first I got yelled at by an assistant principal for being in the wrong hallway at the wrong time, and when I finally made it to the cafeteria, there were no open seats by any of the kids I knew. The few times I approached a friendly looking table with a free seat, someone would shake their head and say the seat was taken. And there was no way I was sitting at any of the boys-only tables. I ended up throwing away my food and going to the library.

The next morning, Dad dropped us off a block from school. Francine stayed with me until we reached the schoolyard, and then bolted to the chorus room. In addition to all the other changes, she'd also decided to join Glee Club.

At lunch, I decided to skip the cafeteria entirely and go to the library instead. I'd brought a granola bar, an apple, and a couple of Dad's *Teen Titans* graphic novels. I figured I could keep this up for at least a few months.

When I got home from school, there was a note from Dad waiting on my bed. *Be ready by 6:00*, it said.

At 6:02, Dad pulled into the driveway and honked the horn.

"Your father's outside," Mom called from the kitchen. "He wants to take you to dinner."

"Be there in a second," Francine yelled back.

"Not you," Mom said a few seconds later, now in our doorway. "Just Maureen."

Francine blinked as she seemed to process Mom's words, but she didn't argue. Maybe she realized that "independence" cut both ways.

Dad took me to my favorite restaurant, Antonio's. He ordered the lasagna, and I ordered shrimp linguini. He even ordered me a Coke, which was supposed to be off-limits during the week.

"So how's school going, kiddo?" Dad always used *kiddo* when he was trying to be hip.

"It could be better."

"I know you're not eating lunch," he said. "And you're not making friends."

"Who told you that?"

"Who do you think?"

"Francine?" I crunched up my nose. "So first she abandons me, and now she rats me out?"

"She didn't abandon you—"

"Look how she dresses. Look what she's reading, the clubs she's joining. It's like she doesn't even want to be my—" I stopped because I could feel my voice wavering.

"It's okay," Dad said softly. "Finish your food. Then we'll talk."

After dinner, Dad steered me toward a nearby bench. It was muggy outside, but he wrapped his arm around me like he was trying to keep me warm. "Do you know why your sister's acting so strange?"

I really hoped this wasn't going to be one of those "when a girl turns into a woman" conversations.

"When you graduated from elementary school, do you know what your class rank was?" After I shook my head, he said, "Three. After the Casey kid and some other girl. Fran was seventh."

"Who cares about rank? It wasn't even a real graduation." *And I can't believe you just called her Fran*, I thought.

"It mattered to her," Dad said. "You've always gotten better grades. You were better at piano—though to be honest, both of you stunk at it—and you always placed better in all the science fairs and school contests." He squeezed my shoulder. "Think about how hard it must feel to always come in second. But now she has a chance to come into her own, without any preconceived notions weighing her down." He took a deep breath. "It wasn't some computer fluke that caused you two to have so many separate classes. Your mother and I requested it. We thought it would be good for both of you."

I pulled away. "What does this have to do with me?"

"Honey, you've got to find your own voice," he said. "You can't do that around your sister. So we figured we'd give you a little nudge."

*More like a shove*, I thought.

"We thought you'd benefit from a little separation," he said. "But we've already talked with the school. We can still change up your schedule, put you and your sister in more classes together. But we'd rather not do that." He turned so he was looking at me. "Just try," he said. "Talk to people. Try to be friendly. You might like it."

Even though it was a school night, Dad kept me out until almost ten. We ate ice cream, then caught a movie. When I got home, Francine was already in bed.

She sat up when I walked in. "I'm sorry for telling Dad—"

"It's okay." I sat down on her bed. Our bookshelf was weighed down with all our medals and trophies. Golds for me. Silvers and bronzes for her. I always thought it was cool the way we won awards. It was like we were the Wonder Twins from that old *Super Friends* cartoon Dad had shown us on YouTube. With our combined powers, no one could stop us.

I took a deep breath. "Are you going to make me call you Fran?"

She cocked her head to the side, and there, in the dark, she really did look like me. "Don't be silly. For you, I'll always be Francine."

★ ★ ★

The next morning, I told Dad that we'd be okay walking to school. Once we got there, I was the first to peel away. "I'll see you in class, okay?"

Francine nodded, and I walked over to a group of boys reading comics. Scott Casey sat at the edge of the group, his face hidden by his book.

"Mind if I sit down?" I asked. I was already pulling out Dad's *Robin: Year One* graphic novel.

Scott looked up at me. "Um . . ."

"We're in the middle of a meeting," one of the kids said.

"Is this a comic book club?" I asked.

The kid snorted. "Manga," he said. "We don't do comic books."

"Robin isn't even a real superhero," another boy said. "He doesn't have any real powers. And he's a sidekick."

"Um . . . okay," I said, my face getting hot. "Never mind."

I walked off. I wasn't sure if I was going to cry, but if so, no way was it going to happen in front of those losers.

I rounded the corner, leaned against the wall, and closed my eyes. There were other kids at school. I could try again. Or try tomorrow. Or even—

"Robin's cool."

I opened my eyes. Scott Casey stood a few feet away, his comic book tucked under his arm. "I mean, his name is kind of lame, but he's really smart. And he knows all these fighting techniques. And he's not even really a sidekick anymore. He's a superhero on his own."

I nodded, trying to piece together why Scott was here. And then I reminded myself that I was supposed to be talking, not just thinking. "Which Robin is your favorite?"

"Tim Drake. Yours?"

"The same."

Scott took a step closer. "I don't even know those guys really well. I just joined their club so I'd have somewhere to sit during lunch. All my other friends have second lunch."

"You could always join me in the library," I said, half-joking.

His eyes widened. "Could I?" he asked. "There's actually another girl in the group that likes superhero comics, as well. Can she tag along? She's really cool."

I nodded. "Sure."

"And I've got a couple of Batman comics in my locker," he said. "Maybe we could trade. I mean . . . if it's okay with you—"

"A trade would be good," I said. The bell rang. "See you in homeroom. And at lunch."

He nodded and walked off. I'd never seen him smile so much before.

I headed toward the building. Francine stood by the door, her arms crossed.

"I saw you and Scott," she said. "What was that all about?"

"Nothing major," I said. "We were just talking."

"Since when did you become a talker?" Francine asked with a grin. "I thought that was my job, remember?"

I grinned back. "Yeah, well maybe it's about time I use my own voice. That is, as long as you can think for yourself."

Francine gave me a playful shove, then we entered the hall-way, side by side. She slowed down as we neared a group of girls from Glee Club, but I kept on toward class.

I didn't even look back.

Mike Winchell

# DANCES AND TALENT SHOWS

**What's your thing? What's that** natural gift that sets you apart? Do you even know yet, or is it still a hidden talent? And what can everyone else do? During your school days, there's no better place to show what you've got than a dance or talent show.

Author-illustrator Don Tate and author Kelly Starling Lyons both know how it feels to wonder what that special talent is, and how thrilling it can be when you finally discover it.

# WIZ KID

was a shy kid who struggled with expressing himself. It was like wearing an invisible straitjacket, a coat of insecurities wrapped so tightly around me that sometimes I couldn't breathe. Breaking loose would prove to be one of the toughest challenges of my life. A challenge that would be met on a yellow brick road with a scarecrow and a tin man.

One day, our seventh-grade music teacher asked our class to divide into groups of three or four and brainstorm ideas for a musical skit. We would perform in front of the entire class. I ended up with Earlee Allen and Zyvonne Robinson, two of the most popular and outgoing girls at school. We chose to perform "Ease on Down the Road," a song from *The Wiz*—although when I say *we*, in reality, it was *they*. As a shy kid, I didn't want to perform anything in front of anyone. The thought made me want to pee my pants.

*The Wiz* was my favorite movie. It was a black retelling of *The Wizard of Oz*, starring entertainers of color who looked like me: Michael Jackson, Diana Ross, Lena Horne, and Richard

Pryor. While watching the movie, I felt a great sense of pride. But pride was no challenge to the constraints of my invisible straitjacket.

At home with my family, I was confident. When my three brothers and I watched *The Wiz* on TV, we bounced along to the music, and I became the lead performer. The bright colors from the movie illuminated our living room, transforming it into a giant dance studio. I sang and danced and acted along; I became Michael Jackson's long-lost twin brother, "easing on down" our raggedy yellow carpet. I was a good dancer, too, no doubt about that. But I wasn't going to shake my booty anywhere other than in the comfort of my home—no way!

I couldn't get out of it, though. I'd have to participate or bring home a bad grade, which would have gotten me into trouble with my parents. After school, Earlee, Zyvonne, and I gathered in the music room to choose parts and begin practicing the scene. Earlee would play the part of Dorothy, while Zyvonne would be the Tin Man. Earlee was a star athlete on the track team, and Zyvonne was active in the Glee Club and chorus. Both were the center of attention at any school gathering. I would play the Scarecrow, though the Cowardly Lion may have been more fitting.

Earlee popped in a cassette tape, and the boom box blasted the song. Earlee and Zyvonne bounced and stepped in sync to the rhythm.

"Come on, Donny," Earlee said, "show us your moves!" But it was no use; that invisible straitjacket tightened its grip around my arms and even my legs. My body went stiff, while my feet were nailed to the floor. My heart beat so loudly, I feared the girls would hear it *thump-thump-thumping* over the music. One by one, other students showed up and joined our impromptu *Wiz* party, and everyone jammed to the funky dance music. Everyone except me. I didn't dance at all that day. I just stood there watching everyone else having fun, wishing I could disappear.

Later that evening, I created a costume from an old pair of overall jeans. Over the knees I sewed on colorful patches of cloth. Under the hem of the pants, I attached dried leaves and brush collected from the gully across the street from our house. The leaves jutted out over my shoes, making a *scritch-scratchy* noise as I walked. A rumpled grocery bag became a hat that I cocked sideways over my mushrooming afro. If nothing else, I'd created an award-winning costume.

On the day of the performances, the school buzzed with excitement as most everyone came dressed in their costumes. Between classes, the hallways resembled the backstage of some great Broadway production. I really wanted to wear my costume like everyone else, but, of course, I didn't want to draw extra attention to myself. I left it at home.

Earlee and Zyvonne were disappointed, but not too much. They knew I was uptight about the whole thing and were happy I didn't stay home, struck with a sudden onset of the Macadamia Nut Flu . . . or something worse. Earlee went all out with her costume. She wore a frilly white dress and red patent leather shoes. She clutched a stuffed white dog that served as Toto. Zyvonne came wrapped from head to toe with aluminum foil—the perfect Tin Man.

★ ★ ★

When the performances began, a rock band dressed like Kiss took to the floor, the players' faces painted crusty white with black eyeliner. Another group performed the Beatles' "Yellow Submarine." On our turn, the three of us lined up in front of the class. Before the music began, Earlee recited her bit about the three of us seeking out the Wiz in hopes of going home, wanting a brain, and getting a heart, and about how we were easing our way on down the road, headed to the beautiful Emerald City. Then she clicked the button on the boom box, and the music began. Earlee and Zyvonne began to dance.

The air around me became as thick as jelly—impossible to breathe—while my legs, frozen stiff all morning, suddenly melted into butter. I tried to jiggle my butt a little, but nothing happened back there. I was so dizzy, I thought I would lose my balance and fall on my face.

That's when I heard the words: "He's so shy." It came from somewhere in the audience. I had no idea who had said it, and it was amazing that I even heard the words over the blaring music.

I hated the word *shy.* I disliked the words *bashful, quiet, timid,* and *self-conscious,* too. They'd all been used to describe me at various points in my life. I felt vulnerable and hurt when others recognized that thing inside of me that I disliked, that thing I had no control over. I felt dumb standing there not doing anything. Then I got angry—at everyone, but mostly at myself. It was time to cut loose from that jacket of shyness. I would no longer be bound.

I looked up from the floor, directly into the audience. Then I imagined myself back home in the living room with my brothers. The music played on, and Dorothy and the Tin Man eased on down the road. But in this version, the Scarecrow led the way—grooving like never before. I danced the Robot, the Watergate, the Poplock. It was nothing like what we had practiced, but it didn't even matter to me.

The song was all of three minutes long, but it could have gone on forever. That was how confident I felt at that moment. Earlee was all smiles.

"I had no idea you could dance like that," she said over the thunderous applause.

"It's the quiet ones you have to look out for!" Zyvonne said. The three of us laughed and slapped high fives.

On that day and during that one skit, I experienced a whole new kind of freedom—the freedom to just be myself. It was a coat of confidence that felt darn good, and I wore it for years to come.

# Don Tate

# DANCE LIKE YOU DRAW

*Oh, please don't get sick*, I beg myself. My stomach tightens like a vice. It's dinnertime when Moms announces her plan to sign me up for cotillion class.

"AKA a frilly charm school for uppity folks," Dad says. Moms glares at him, annoyed.

"It's not a charm school; it's an etiquette program. It'll be good for Silas," Moms says. "He'll learn social skills, and it may help him to overcome his shy ways."

*Shy ways.* I hate it whenever Moms say that about me. My brain races for a response, but nothing. I pick over my food, plunging my finger deep into my salad. I fish out a grape.

"Only babies eat with their fingers," Moms says. "Perfect example of how a cotillion program will help you with manners." Then Moms smiles so wide, her face almost splits. "Think about it like this, Silas. On the last day, you'll get to dance with a pretty girl in a lavish dress at some swanky ballroom party."

I almost puke my brains out right there.

★ ★ ★

On the first day of cotillion class, I drag myself out of the car, lugging two bottles of soda. Then I trudge across the parking lot toward the church, where the seventh-grade classes are held. It's warm outside for early January in Austin, Texas, and I feel myself sweating around the collar. Hot air and frazzled nerves are not a good mix.

Moms whips past in a swift breeze, balancing a tower of donut boxes in her arms. She glances back at me before disappearing into the church. Moms is a volunteer chaperone, of course — aka a spy. She'll gather intelligence information on my use of good manners. But most of all, she'll watch to see if I'm acting shy — which makes me want to crawl under a rock and hide. Inside the church, the fellowship hall, which doubles as a basketball court, is dim and reeks of bread mold and Windex. Kids mill around quietly; no one seems excited to be here — well, except for the parent chaperones, of course.

I feel uncomfortable and self-conscious in this too-tight dress shirt and suffocating tie. Not to mention the wedgie-inducing khaki pants Moms made me wear. My favorite hoodie and jeans are not allowed at cotillion class. Uppity folks — Dad was right.

An elderly man in a dark suit clutches a microphone and asks everyone to sit. I find a chair in a corner of the room and slink down into it. I pull out my phone and Instagram a selfie. "Charm school is lame," I write below the pic. When the man notices me tapping at my phone, he comes over.

"Good morning, Mr., uh" — he stops, examines my name tag — "Mr. Silas Taylor. Would you mind joining everyone else at the tables?" His large hand points toward a group of about thirty kids, who are now staring at me. My heart races, my face is hot. Moms watches with worry. I pick up my things and sit across the table from a group of boys.

That's when I see *her* at a table on the far side of the room — Andi Burke. At school, they call her Loud Andi, because she speaks thirty decibels louder than everyone else. Loud Andi's voice is like a jackhammer. She's confident, taller than most boys, which, I guess, most girls are in middle school. But Loud Andi has bigger biceps than any boy I know. One time at lunch, Loud Andi challenged Johnny Morris, captain of the wrestling team, by demanding he give over his lunch. When he refused, he ended up wearing meatballs and noodles all over his face (after he picked his face up off the floor). Quickly, I avert my eyes away from Andi. But not in time. She catches my gaze and returns a sour glare. I don't know why, but Loud Andi has never liked me — or anyone, for that matter.

From a podium, the man in the dark suit speaks again. Says his name is Mr. Oxley, founder of the cotillion program — the Hill Country School of Etiquette. He's a short man with a swayback posture. Carries his nose high in the air like an old-time radio antenna. He's plump with a round face and white beard. If his suit were red, he might get mistaken for a remote control Santa Claus.

"Youth of today," Mr. Oxley begins his speech, his nose seeming to transmit an electromagnetic wave, "with your duck-face selfies. You think everything is all about you." He looks directly at me. I jam my phone deeper into my pocket. "Over the course of this program," he says, "you will learn to consider others."

After a long lecture where he outlines his plans to torture us over the next few weeks, we break into small groups. Girls are on one side of the room, boys on the other. The girls learn about things like sitting, standing, walking, pivoting. Boys work on things like making proper introductions and hand shaking. Mr. Oxley demonstrates the proper hand-shaking protocol: Stand tall. Look the other person in the eye. Smile. Don't shake any more than three pumps (from the elbow). When Mr. Oxley asks me to demonstrate a handshake, I look at the floor. Then I slowly raise my hand. We shake. "You're not looking at me," he says, "and your hand is as lifeless as a dead fish."

I'm embarrassed again. To redeem myself, I reach my hand out for another shake. This time, I squeeze so hard, the veins in my thumb pop out.

"Squeezing too hard is disrespectful," Mr. Oxley says, snatching his hand away abruptly. Who'd've thought that shaking hands could require so much brainpower?

Next, Mr. Oxley and a lady from the school prepare to dance. She faces him, and they join hands in an awkward and boxy embrace. The music begins, and they demonstrate some kind of stiff-as-a-tree dance Mr. Oxley calls the waltz—"One-two-three, one-two-three, one-two-three," they count rather loudly, stepping to and fro in a square pattern. Apparently, Mr. Oxley has never seen the YouTube Hip-Hop channel, because this waltz seems less like dancing and more like counting.

Everyone watches. Some even giggle. The counting dance ends, and then Mr. Oxley directs us to form two lines, side by side — boys in one line, girls in the other. I'm tired and ready to go home. But the day is not over yet. "Ladies and gentlemen," Mr. Oxley says, "it's time for you to dance. Whoever stands next to you will be your dance partner for this next session." My body turns to stone; I'm afraid to look and see who's standing next to me.

"Oh, great," a gruff voice says, "I gotta dance with Silas Taylor?" I recognize that voice.

Loud Andi Burke.

I almost puke my brains out.

Loud Andi and I shake hands and introduce ourselves the way we were instructed. The music begins. The chaperones keep watch. Other couples begin the counting dance: *one-two-three, one-two-three, one-two-three* . . . But Loud Andi and I just stand there. Her hands are balled up on her hips, and her laser eyes are boring a hole through my head. My legs are pillars of ice, and my face is on fire. I can't move. I can't breathe. I definitely can't dance. Loud Andi howls with laughter, and everyone looks.

And that's when I do it. I get sick. Right then and there. All over the floor. All over Andi's dress.

"You big—ah!" She charges into the restroom.

★ ★ ★

At home I plow my head under my pillow. I try to think about good things, like fishing or camping on the weekends with Dad, or the time I won the poster contest in art class. Good memories blot out the bad. What happened earlier today was definitely not good. After puking all over Loud Andi, she promised to snap my skinny body into two pieces if I ever came within spitting distance of her again. And she'll do it, too! I don't doubt that for a second.

A whiff of Moms's homemade pizza blurs the image of Loud Andi beating me like drumsticks. It's pizza night, when Moms and Dad and I normally chow down on my favorite pineapple-bacon-sausage pie and watch *America's Best Dance Crew* on TV. But after what happened at cotillion class, I'm not in the mood for anything to do with dancing.

I drag myself out of bed and over to my desk. In my sketch pad, I begin drawing another comic. Sly Jamma—my alter ego—is a masked superhero I created in art class. With his mighty Sword of Doom, Sly can do just about anything. He's big and brave, a smooth talker. Everything I am not. Today Sly faces off with the scariest of villains anyone could ever think of: Loud Andi Burke and Mean Mr. Oxley. *Zow! Zing! Kaboom!*—Sly annihilates them with one mighty zap. All of my problems seem to dissolve when Sly Jamma jumps into action.

"Silas?" Moms asks, knocking at my door. "Are you okay?

"I'm fine," I say, putting the last touches on my comic. Moms pushes the door open.

"You're missing the show," she says, all giddy. "Tonight they're deciding who will advance to—"

My comic grabs her attention. She stops talking and picks up my sketch pad.

"Wow," she says. "With talent like this, you can do anything—draw, dance, whatever you set your mind to."

I stuff my sketch pad and pencils back into my desk and tramp downstairs for pizza.

Cotillion classes drudge on for a couple more weeks. At the next session, we learn how a formal dinner is served. Each place setting has enough bowls and silverware to feed an entire family of nine. Then Mr. Oxley teaches us how to tie a double Windsor knot, an overly complicated way of tying a necktie. Then he discusses the importance of speaking clearly on the phone, instructing us to silence them while at the symphony or museum. "Definitely no selfies," he says, glancing my way.

Once again, Mr. Oxley asks us to form two lines. Remembering what happened last time, my stomach knots into one of those double Windsors.

We line up, but this time I'm standing next to a girl I haven't seen here before: Livi Anderson. She's new to this program, but not new to me. Livi is in my art class at school. She often compliments my artwork. Sometimes I create special drawings just for her.

The problem is, whenever I open my mouth to speak to Livi, the words clog like a hairball in a bathroom sink. Nothing sensible comes out. Regardless, Livi is probably my only friend. I like her, and I think she likes me, too. Today I feel more at ease knowing she'll be my dance partner.

"Watch out for Puke Face," Loud Andi barks. Several other kids in line snicker, but Livi does not.

She whispers to me: "If you dance like you draw, you will shut Ms. Megamouth up." I laugh out loud for the first time since cotillion classes began.

The music starts—*one-two-three, one-two-three, one-two-three*—and we dance. My legs are stiff, but I manage to move them. Livi and I are a full arm's-length apart, but at this moment, I feel closer to her than anyone else in the world.

On the next beat, Mr. Oxley raises his hand. It's time to rotate partners. I turn, face another girl—Taryn. We dance—*one-two-three, one-two-three, one-two-three*. Then it's time to rotate partners again—Alysha. We dance—*one-two-three, one-two-three, one-two-three*. It's not the same dancing with the other two girls, though. When I dance with Livi, rockets launch inside of me.

★ ★ ★

After class, I want to ask Livi to be my partner at the cotillion—the formal dance party at the end of the program. As she and her dad prepare to leave the fellowship hall, I yell, "Wait . . . Livi!" Words so clear I surprise even myself. I zoom across the room.

"Silas?" she asks, standing there with her dad.

My hands wander through my pockets for something that isn't there. I try to speak, but my lips are paralyzed. A few blurry words manage to tumble out and tangle with one another.

"I need . . . would you . . . the dance . . . you know . . . but . . ." My mind is empty; no more words come out. If this was a drawing, I would erase this entire image.

Livi touches my hand. Her dad looks away. "I would be happy to be your dance partner at the ball," she says. Livi understands my babble. I'm the luckiest guy in the world.

★　★　★

The ballroom is amazing at cotillion! It's much bigger than the fellowship hall at the church. Large wooden doors and gold-painted columns sweep high toward the ornate ceiling. White-covered tables span the room as far as I can see. The chairs are wrapped in white cloth and tied in the back with a bow. And the napkins are something else, too—they are folded intricately to look like black swans. A large, bowl-shaped chandelier hangs from the ceiling. It is covered with crystals and ringed with bright lights. It looks like an alien spaceship policing the event. One misstep and—zap!—someone is dead.

I scan the room looking for Livi and see my reflection in a mirror. Black tuxedo. Dark, shiny shoes. Afro blown out so long over my thin body, I look like a walking umbrella. And then I see Livi.

She is wearing her hair down. It's long and frames her perfect face like a classic painting in a museum. Her arms are covered with white gloves that stretch to her elbows. Her white

**183**

dress is tied at the waist with a silky blue ribbon and falls softly in layers just below her knees. But beneath her knees—or at least her right knee—her leg is in a plaster cast covered with mesh the color of a tangerine.

"I broke my leg at softball practice," she says. "The cast doesn't exactly match my dress, but orange is my favorite color."

Livi explains how we can still eat dinner together, just not dance. I'm numb. The room spins. Everything moves in slow motion.

Dinner begins. Livi sits at my right; Loud Andi at my left. I figure that since Loud Andi is not my dinner partner, I don't need to talk to her. She sees differently, though. She's like a yakking machine turned up to full blast—she won't shut up! Every time I try to talk to Livi, Loud Andi cuts in. I wonder where her date is; who is her dance partner? Next thing, Loud Andi turns and stabs her fork into my salad. I guess all those sessions about grace and poise and table manners were wasted on a girl like her.

Mr. Oxley scurries over to our table, a dark fog seeming to follow him. "Being that Miss Livi is incapacitated this evening, and being that Miss Andi has no date, she will be your dance partner."

Loud Andi's eyes bunch up into an angry frown. So do Livi's.

I almost puke my brains out right there.

The lights dim and the crowd applauds. It's time to dance. Our table is called to the floor first. I look at Livi. Her frown disappears. She leans in, whispers in my ear, "Dance like you draw." More rockets launch inside of me again.

Couples enter the wooden dance floor. It's polished so shiny, I can see my reflection. It's an image I haven't seen before. I look assured, brave, like Sly Jamma.

Loud Andi and I clasp hands. She leans in. "You'd better not mess up and embarrass me," she says, crunching my hand in a death grip.

My blood races. My body temperature explodes. But this time, Loud Andi's threats do not scare me. They make me angry; they pump me up.

From a nearby table, Moms snaps a picture. Dad beams with pride.

The soft roll of a piano precedes the *um-pa-pa — um-pa-pa — um-pa-pa* bouncy music.

I look up from the floor — away from Loud Andi — and imagine myself at home in my room with a pad of paper, a pencil, and my hero Sly Jamma holding his sword.

And then, just like Livi said, I dance like I draw. I waltz and fox-trot and tango and swing. All the dances we learned. I may not perform them perfectly, but it feels so good to cut loose and just be myself. Loud Andi struggles to keep in step.

*Swoosh!* — my mighty Sword of Doom crushes Loud Andi, which I'm sure would please Sly Jamma to no end. Moms, Dad, and Livi are pleased, too. When I spin around on the dance floor, I see their faces all glowing with pride.

# Kelly Starling Lyons

## WHAT REALLY HAPPENED

# THE COOL IN ME

When I walked through the doors of my Pittsburgh middle school, I felt awkward and out of place. I was a skinny sixth grader with too-big glasses and braids crisscrossed on my head little-girl style. I gaped at the hugeness of the school. I marveled at the fashions of kids who looked like they had stepped off the cover of a teen magazine. It felt like everyone rocked designer jeans like Jordache, Sergio Valente, and Gloria Vanderbilt, while I wore no-names from a discount department store.

My favorite pair had an embroidered patch of skates on a back pocket with real laces you could tie. I couldn't wait to show them off, but when I got to school it took just one comment to make me wish I had left them on the rack.

"Where did you get *those* from?" a girl said with a sneer.

It wasn't her words that stung, it was her tone. Oozing with scorn, it made me feel foolish for thinking I would get compliments. I pretended like I didn't hear her question, but my shoulders slumped for the rest of the day.

I was in the gifted program, could spell like a champ, and was the only girl in the percussion section of the jazz ensemble. But I wanted more. I ached to be cool.

When tryouts were announced for cheerleaders for the Mini-Globes basketball team, I signed up. I had no dance lessons or experience cheering, but I had drive. I looked at the other girls, who seemed so poised and perfect, and anxiously waited for my turn. I stilled my nerves by going over the moves in my head. I had the motions and chant down:

Strawberry Shortcake, Huckleberry Pie, V-I-C-T-O-R-Y.

"Next."

I was up. I gave the cheer my all. I don't know if I didn't muster enough team spirit or jump high enough at the end, but it was a pass. I left humbled and determined to try something else.

My next mission was diving into my secret desire to be a hip-hop queen. Breakdancing, deejaying, rapping, I wanted to do it all. I watched in amazement kids who broke out cardboard and hit windmills and back spins. I tried to scratch records and spin on my knee in my bedroom. I wrote raps about school, hanging out with my friends and cousins, and battling rappers like Roxanne Shanté. Some buddies and I pretended to be a crew, the Glamorous Gang, named after Sheila E's hit "The Glamorous Life." I was Lady K.

I daydreamed about spitting rhymes that made kids throw their hands in the air, and imagined popping and locking like I was an extra on the movie Breakin'. I even went to school one day armed with Mom-approved rhymes to lyrically take down some boys who were a pain. Ready to spar, I called one a roller skate and said I wanted to use his head to do a figure eight. Supercorny, but it cracked him up and me, too. I had imagination, but an MC I was not.

But something happened as I tried and failed at cheerleading and rap—I started feeling good about who I was. My cool came from making up secret codes and passing notes to my best friend, Nikki, between classes and sharing our own special jokes that made us giggle and lock arms.

My cool came from making good grades and being selected to be part of a special science club. Mr. Scott, a teacher who made learning the meaning of inertia as awesome as watching a new music video, was my hero: "Objects have a tendency to resist the changes in motion," he rapped while we kept time with cowbells and tambourines.

My cool came from Mr. Powell's band room, where I played synthesizer. In Jazz Ensemble, I jammed in the back with the guys who played drums, electric piano, and bass. Mr. Powell, brilliant, quirky, and exacting, pushed us to improvise and shine in solos. We played songs like "Sailing" and "Ride Like the Wind" by Christopher Cross and performed for students around the city. Then, one day, Mr. Powell wrote "Kelly's Blues," a song just for me.

Even in the out-of-date black tuxedo pants and gold butterfly collar shirt that was our uniform, I felt as smooth as Herbie Hancock playing "Rockit." My fingers danced across the keys during my moment in the spotlight as my friends and family cheered me on.

As I came into myself, I discovered my style groove, too. Who needed designer gear when you had creativity? I mixed flowered jeans with my mom's pastel ruffled shirts and wore cha-cha skirts with leggings and fluorescent high tops with a hat slung on my back. I rocked my glasses and sported hairdos that felt just right. I still heard an occasional snarky comment, but louder than that I could hear my own voice telling me to raise my head to the sky and strut. By the end of eighth grade, I didn't need anyone's approval. I was the kind of cool only I could be.

## Kelly Starling Lyons

THE STORY

# THE JACKET

pushed through the steel door into Three Rivers Middle School and felt as puny as a guppy in an ocean. The winding hallway streamed with kids, some nervous and shy like me, some with teen swagger and style. Friends laughed as they plastered the insides of their lockers with patterned paper, mirrors, and stickers and posters of singers like Michael Jackson and Madonna. Everything seemed louder and freer than elementary. No walking in line here. Kids owned these halls.

Inside my sixth-grade classroom, I hoped to see a familiar face. But I knew going to a school with kids from around the city made that a long shot. I looked and came up empty. It took just a few minutes to figure out which girls would be popular. Tonya Prince and her crew rocked Jheri curls and feathered hair. The labels of their designer jeans—Gloria Vanderbilt, Sergio Valente, and Jordache—flashed as they strutted around the room. Looking at them made me wish I'd picked something else to wear.

With a bow in my hair, patent leather Mary Janes, and a new-to-me fuchsia jumper from Moms's "special store," I knew I stood out. And sure enough, when we changed classes, Tonya zeroed in on me.

"Are you lost?" she asked with a sneer.

"No." Weird question. We were both going to the same place—math across the hall.

"I think you're lost. Church is a block down the street."

Her friends high-fived and cackled. I sighed and trudged to my desk. It was going to be a long year.

But when Mrs. Richardson started reading word problems for us to solve, I perked up and sat taller. In elementary school, buddies called me Encyclopedia Brown because I could figure out anything. Every time, my hand was the first one up. Kids looked impressed. I just knew I had it made. Until I heard a nasty whisper.

"Know-it-all," Tonya spat just loud enough for me to hear. Her girls giggled.

When Mrs. Richardson read the next question, I kept my hand down, though I had figured out the answer in my head. I studied her black-and-gold Steelers pennant when she asked for a volunteer to solve a problem on the board. As soon as the bell rang, I grabbed my notebook and pencil case and rushed to the door.

"Don't let them get to you," a girl with a puffy ponytail and braces whispered as she hustled alongside me. "My mom said girls only tease you when they're jealous."

Jealous? Of me? I looked at her and smiled.

"Thanks," I said. "I'm Cassie."

"Zoe."

"What do you have next?"

"Band," she said.

"No way," I said, grinning. "Me, too."

We entered the sunny room filled with rows of black metal music stands. Flutes, clarinets, and horns beckoned from tables. Mr. Jamison called over kids with no experience to figure out what would be a good fit. Zoe got flute—something I always wanted to play. I had been taking piano lessons since I was five, so it was a no-brainer. Keyboard for me. Zoe said she always wanted to learn how to play piano. We giggled and promised to teach each other.

At lunchtime, I patted a seat next to me for Zoe to sit. We poked at the meatloaf covered with gravy, which oozed like brown slime on our trays, and we grimaced at each other. We took a couple of bites, then stuck with the applesauce, green beans, and tater tots.

"Ready?" I said.

Zoe nodded.

We dumped our trays and headed outside to the courtyard. Music from the local radio station pumped through speakers. A crowd formed around a group of boys rapping back and forth, trading rhymes like they were Run-D.M.C. We rocked along with their flow and cheered when someone delivered a zinger. Then came the dancers. Kids popped and locked, did the worm on the grass, and spread out cardboard and nailed moves that made them look like spinning tops.

Tonya and her girls stood along the side bopping back and forth. But they were no match for Zoe. She tilted her head to the right, and her body followed like a snake. She tilted her head to the left and brought her body back the other way.

"You got skills," I said, making a mental note to work on that dance move when I got home.

"So do you. You take dance, too?"

"Nope," I said. "Just love it."

While we jammed, I didn't see Ricky Holmes, one of the cutest boys in class, walk up alongside us.

"Cassie, take off your glasses for a minute," he said.

"What?"

"Just take them off."

I slipped them off my face and watched his features blur. Ricky smiled.

"You have pretty eyes."

He walked away. I grinned and quickly slid my glasses back on.

Tonya, standing in earshot, frowned and looked me up and down. She had seen and heard everything.

★ ★ ★

Whenever she could after that, Tonya took a swipe at me. She was there when I dropped my books.

"Butterfingers," she called.

She was there when I broke the arm of my glasses and had to squint throughout the day.

"Look at Miss Magoo," she said.

She was there when I checked out the poster in the cafeteria inviting kids to try out for the talent show. You could rap, dance, sing, play an instrument. The winner would win $25 and a homework pass.

"I know *you're* not thinking about entering," Tonya said.

Her buddies yukked it up behind her.

That did it. I hadn't really thought about entering. But instantly, my mind was made up. Not only was I going to enter, I was going to take it all. I didn't want to win. I *had* to.

At lunch, I told Zoe my idea.

"I don't know, Cassie," she said, chomping on a French fry. "Have you ever been in a talent show before?"

"No, but I've played in recitals. Same thing."

"Not really," she said, running her tongue over her braces. "I've been in dance performances, too. But this will be in front of the whole school."

My stomach plunged at the words *whole school*. I felt like I was on a runaway roller coaster racing toward disaster. What if I messed up? Instead of instant fame, it would be epic shame. I gulped and kept talking.

"Come on, Zoe. We can do it together," I said, hoping my words would convince her. And *me*, too. "Let's come up with something great and shock everybody."

Zoe ran her tongue over her braces as she thought things through. Then smiled and nodded.

"Okay, I'm in."

"Really? All right!"

Now, we just had to figure out what our act would be. For the rest of the day, I tried to think of something. I could play piano while Zoe danced. No, that was too ordinary. We could dance together to a song by our favorite singer, Michael Jackson. Or we could . . . I thought about the rapping and breakdancing in the courtyard during lunch. Everybody loved it. What if Zoe and I rapped and danced? It would be totally unexpected and cool. There was no way we could lose. I could picture kids up on their feet, waving their hands from side to side.

*Say ho!* I imagined myself yelling, lost in my daydream.

*Ho!* the crowd called back.

"Earth to Cassie," snapped Mrs. Richardson. I realized I was back in the classroom—all eyes on me. "I just asked you to solve the problem on the board."

"Sorry, Mrs. Richardson."

As I walked to the front of the room, I heard Tonya snicker. I didn't even care. Let her laugh. I had a plan.

That weekend, I used my allowance to buy a book about hip-hop. I tried to spin on my knee in my bedroom and make a wave travel from my fingertips on one hand to the other side. But I didn't stress about the moves—I knew Zoe would make sure our dance looked good. My job was to come up with the rap. I wrote and rewrote, spitting rhymes to my mom, little brother, whoever would listen. I served the lines and pushed myself harder when they fell flat. It was too late to back down. I *had* to make it work.

Zoe and I had a sleepover before Friday's talent show. Our

moms surprised us with matching jackets. We could decorate them any way we wanted. We used an airbrush, rhinestones, iron-ons, the works. Zoe slid on her jacket, spun around, and struck a pose.

"What do you think?"

"We're gonna look good."

*Just as good as Tonya and her crew*, I thought. Maybe better because we hooked these up ourselves. Now, all we had to do was win.

But as the days got closer, I felt more and more sick. I knew the rhymes and the moves, but I didn't know if I could do it. Who was I kidding? I wasn't a rapper. I kept thinking about what Zoe had said: *in front of the whole school*. I could feel eyes, hundreds of eyes, staring up at me. I saw Tonya and her girls waiting to pick apart every move.

"You can do this," I told myself, when the worries tried to rule.

★ ★ ★

I thought I had the jitters beat until the big day came. I peeked through the curtains and saw the auditorium packed with kids ready to watch the show. So many faces, so many eyes. The closer it got to our turn, the more I wanted to run.

"I'll be right back," I mumbled, trying to swallow down the bitter taste rising in my throat.

"Just two more acts and then us," Zoe said. "Hurry!"

I raced from backstage, hoping I didn't throw up before I got to the bathroom. When I rushed inside, I heard gagging coming from a stall. I swallowed down my own sick feeling and knocked on the door.

"Are you okay?"

"Just leave me alone," a shaky voice answered.

"Wait here. I'll get a teacher."

"No," the voice moaned, and the stall door slowly opened.

There was Tonya with tears falling down her face and a stain on her neon yellow shirt.

"What are you looking at?!" she screamed when she saw it was me and slammed the door. It bounced back open.

Her face was blotchy. Her lips trembled in anger, or maybe it was fear. I took off my jacket, the one I worked so hard on, the one I couldn't wait to show off, and held it out to her.

"If you zip it up, no one will know."

Tonya sniffed, and stared at me with a confused look on her face like she was trying to figure out if this was some kind of trick.

"Why are you being nice to me?" she finally said, wiping her eyes.

"I don't know." I tried not to think about how nasty she had been. It could have been me who threw up. I stretched out the jacket again. "Want it or not?"

She took it and looked down.

"Thanks."

I turned to leave and gasped when I suddenly remembered Zoe's plea to hurry back.

"I gotta go," I said, rushing toward the door.

"Cassie, please don't tell anybody," Tonya pleaded to my back.

"I won't," I called out, letting the door flap behind me. I raced down the hallway. When I made it to backstage, Zoe was in freak-out mode.

"Where were you?!"

"Sorry," I huffed, trying to catch my breath.

"Where's your jacket?"

"I don't have it. But it's okay. I'm ready."

Nerves gone, I danced on stage and did my best. I forgot a couple of moves, but kept going just like I do when I forget a note while playing piano. We delivered the lines I wrote to try to earn some cred. The audience laughed in the right places and clapped when we danced. When it was over, Zoe and I high-fived and then exchanged a look. It was fun, but I knew we wouldn't be doing that again. Next time, we wouldn't enter the talent show just to score some cool points.

Tonya bounced back and killed it. She and her crew won second place for their hip-hop routine. Zoe and I came in third.

After it was over, kids surrounded Tonya and her girls and Zoe and me, saying how awesome we were. But Tonya kept looking my way. When I smiled at her, she came over.

"Congratulations," I said.

"Thanks," she said, seeming suddenly shy, "for everything." She leaned in and whispered: "I'll give your jacket back tomorrow."

"Why is she wearing your jacket?" Zoe asked when Tonya walked away.

I shrugged and changed the subject. If someone heard about Tonya's accident, it wouldn't come from me.

Tonya and I shared a secret, but we never really became friends. She stopped teasing. We smiled at each other sometimes. That was good enough.

Zoe and I made a pact. Pinkies clasped, we pledged to be ourselves. We were band girls who loved to dance, get good grades, and create our own style. That was the kind of cool only we could be.

Mike Winchell

# Bus Ride

**The end of the school day is finally** here. But now you have to get home, and that means you're in for a trip on the bus. And the thing about the school bus is, almost anything can happen inside.

Authors Steve Sheinkin and Ellen Yeomans share their more memorable bus rides with us, and then take those experiences and morph them into some pretty interesting stories.

# Steve Sheinkin

## WHAT REALLY HAPPENED

# THE UNFORTUNATE SCHOOL BUS INCIDENT

So I'm sorry, but this is gross.

I had just started at this new school, and didn't know anyone yet. I was always pretty shy, so it took me a while to make friends. On the bus to and from school, I would sit alone, on the right side, by a window, and try to lay low, remain unnoticed.

I should explain that at age ten I was superskinny, superfreckly, and had this enormous head of reddish-brown curly hair. Basically, it looked like I was wearing a clown's wig. The kids on the bus called it a nest and thought it was hilarious to pretend to check it for birds. My mother insisted my hair looked handsome, and whenever I was forced to go with her to her hairdresser other women would sigh and say stuff like, "I'd spend all day in the beauty parlor for hair like that!" Which I guess kind of explains why kids found it so funny. But that's not really the point.

The point is I hated riding the bus and I sat alone.

But there was at least one person on that bus worse off

than me. The driver. He was this enormously obese guy who was wedged into his seat, and for some reason he always wore this thick, Russian-style fur hat, even on hot days. So he was always very red and sweaty. But on the afternoon this unpleasant little story takes place, I got on the bus to go home and noticed that he was looking pale, almost see-through. It was obvious he was sick.

I went to my usual seat. On the back of the seat in front of me some kids had scrawled very bad—I mean, artistically incompetent—obscene drawings of what were supposed to be teachers in our school. We were about halfway to my house when the bus driver pulled over. He picked up his radio and said, "Eighty-four to base." The dispatcher came on, and our driver explained that he was feeling sick. The dispatcher asked him to try to finish the route. Our driver said he'd try.

He seriously did not look well.

So we continued. But at one of the next stops, just as a few kids were walking down the steps, he leaned toward the door and opened his giant mouth and vomited amounts I didn't know were possible. The first fountain splattered the leg of one of the girls getting off, and she screamed like she was being murdered.

I watched it all from my seat. There were only a couple other kids still on the bus, and we were dying from the stench, holding our noses and mouths to keep from puking ourselves.

Finally the driver lifted his radio again and said, in this really sad voice, "Eighty-four to base. I just got sick all over the bus." The dispatcher said he'd send a new bus to pick us up. He sounded angry.

Then we all just sat there. We asked to wait outside, but the driver said he couldn't let us, for some reason having to do with the school's liability insurance.

We waited for what seemed like an eternity. It became a whole thing, a pathetic little reality show— kids from the neighborhood came up to look at us and to see the mess on the stairs. Some shouted about how gross it was, and they laughed at the driver and at those of us still stuck on the bus. The driver seemed really upset. He put his head in his hands. His shoulders shook a little, like he was crying.

Finally we heard this burst of laughter from the kids outside. The new bus was coming, and it was one of the short ones. The kids found that hilarious. The short bus parked behind us, and the new driver got out and came around and opened the emergency doors in the back of our bus. And one by one, we jumped out the back and got on the short bus.

Only the bus driver stayed on the bus. We left him there. I don't know how he got home.

Of course, this became a famous incident in our school for a little while, and people asked me to tell the story a lot. I loved the attention, and got a lot of laughs. And I'm kind of ashamed to admit that it was only later, many years later, that I started to think about what that day must have been like for the bus driver.

And I wished someone had been on his side.

# Steve Sheinkin

# THROW UP

Sometimes I can tell when something bad's about to happen. I once said that my sister was going to get hurt, and that night at dinner she told everyone she had a raisin up her nose. No one believed her, but she kept saying it so my dad got some tweezers. She cried because the tweezers poked her, but my dad said, "Sit still," and he really did pull out a raisin. It had blood on it.

I had that feeling again when I got on the bus this day. Our bus driver is very fat. He wears a fur hat all the time like the kind they wear in Russia. His face is always red and sweaty. No one has ever seen him stand up. This day, his face was even extra red and sweaty, and you could tell he was sick.

I sat in my same seat in the middle of the bus on the right side. On the back of the seat in front of me were naked drawings of different teachers from our school. No one ever sat next to me, except sometimes for a little while to touch my hair and say they were looking to see if there were any birds living in the curls, because they said it was like a nest.

It was a hot day, but we couldn't open the windows anymore. Too many kids stuck their heads out like dogs do. "You might get your head chopped off," the driver said, "and then I'll be in big trouble."

When there were still seven kids on the bus, the driver pulled over. "This isn't a stop," one kid said. "The bus driver is lost again." The kids all laughed.

The bus driver picked up his radio and said, "Eighty-four to base."

The radio crackled, and a guy said, "Come in, Eighty-four."

The driver said, "Vic, I don't feel so good."

The guy asked, "What's the matter, Clark?"

"I think it's the flu. Remember I felt dizzy before? Now I feel a little nauseous."

The guy asked if he could finish the route, and the driver said he thought so.

The next stop was a street where three kids got off, and the stop after that was a street where the rest of the kids but me get off. We were at that stop. I was watching the bus driver. He was still sweaty, but his face was white instead of red. His eyes were closed. His lips were moving even though he wasn't saying anything. The last girl was at the top of the steps when he leaned toward the door. I thought he was trying to stand, but he didn't take off his seat belt. He started throwing up. The girl screamed, and jumped down the steps, but some got on her leg. It was orange and creamy, and there was a lot of it. It made a milky spilling sound. He threw up four times. It dripped down the steps and fell out onto the street.

It looked funny, but then I smelled it and I almost had to throw up, too. I covered my mouth and nose and lay down on my seat. I heard the bus driver cough and spit. Then he threw up a little bit more. I took deep breaths through my mouth, which is good for not smelling, but I could taste it a little. Then I looked up over the seat. He picked up the radio and said, "Eighty-four to base," and spit onto the stairs while he was waiting.

The guy came on and said, "What now, Eighty-four?"

The driver said, "I just got sick on the bus."

"What? What are you talking about?"

The driver said, "Yeah, on the steps and everything. It's a real mess."

The guy said, "Oh man, Clark," and he sounded angry. "Is there anyone still there?"

The driver looked up in the mirror and saw me. "One kid."

"Oh, man," the guy said. "Wait there. I'll send someone to get him."

And then we just sat there. He said I could open my window, and I did. I stuck my head out and I could see the hill my house was on.

"Can I walk home?" I asked.

"I can't let you."

"Why not?" I asked.

"Because of insurance reasons."

I stuck my head out the window again and breathed the air.

A little kid rode by on his bike and asked what happened. "The bus driver threw up five times," I said.

"Why don't you get off?"

I said, "Insurance."

I looked out the window for three minutes, and the little kid kept sitting there on his bike watching the bus. Then I heard the bus driver's seat squeak. He was standing up. No one had ever seen him stand up before. He looked at me and said, "You mind if I come back there? The stench is killing me."

I said okay, and he walked past me and sat in the very back seat with his legs out in the aisle, because he wouldn't fit the regular way.

"The other bus should be here soon," he said. He face was back to being red. He shook his head and said, "I'm very sorry about that." When he talked there was a string of yellow spit between his lips that stretched up and down but didn't break.

I looked at the naked pictures on the back of the seat in front of me, because if I looked at him I might have to talk to him more. I wondered if he was going to let me go out the emergency exit in the back—or would I have to walk through the throw-up? I could even jump out the window if they would let me.

I thought I heard a bus coming and I looked up, but it was a truck. When the truck went by it was loud, and when it left I could hear the bus driver breathing. He was taking breaths every second, and his nose sniffled. I thought he was laughing at first, but he kept going for so long, and nobody ever laughs that many times. I was afraid to turn around and look at him. I thought he might get mad or embarrassed. But I turned a little bit and pretended to be looking out the window, and I could see him, because one thing I can do is see sideways. He was leaning forward with his arms crossed and his head facing down. His eyes were closed, but tears were coming out of them. He was shaking a little. I turned back around before he could see me.

Then I heard talking from outside the bus. I looked out and there was the little kid, and also the three kids from that bus stop. The girl had on new pants. They looked at the throw-up on the steps and then ran away, laughing. They came back and walked around the bus and saw the bus driver in the back.

"What's he crying about?" one of them asked.

"I don't know," I said out the window.

"Why don't you get off?"

"I'm not allowed," I said. They laughed, and two other kids came on bikes from down the road. Soon there were a lot of kids outside the bus, and some of them were even in junior high. They walked all around the bus and kept shouting to me, "Do you like it in there?" "Does it smell good?" "Are you going to cry, too?"

I didn't answer, but they kept asking.

The bus driver wasn't making noise anymore. I looked back and his head was resting in his hands. His fingers were fat and they covered his whole face. He wasn't shaking. The kids outside started shouting and I looked, and there was another bus coming. It was a little one. It stopped behind us, and the other driver got out. The kids told him that our bus driver threw up, and he said he knew all about it. They showed him the throw-up, and he made a face and said, "That's disgusting."

The new driver walked to the back of the bus and opened the emergency door. The kids were around him, looking in. I bent down to pick up my bag from the floor.

"What's his name?" the new driver asked.

Someone said my name was *Nesty* and someone said *Stevie* and someone said *Stephen*, and the new driver said, "Come on, Stephen, I'm gonna take you home."

I had my bag on my lap. All the kids were looking at me. Our driver pulled his legs in so I could get by. But I didn't get up.

"Let's go. Hurry up!" the new driver said.

"Maybe he died," a kid said.

Another kid said, "Maybe it's past his bedtime, and he went to sleep."

They all laughed. I turned around and looked at the seat in front of me.

"What's your problem?" the new driver asked. "Don't you want me to take you home?" I didn't answer, so he asked our driver, "Clark, what's this kid's problem?" Our driver didn't say anything. The new driver said, "Stephen, are you coming out or not? It really doesn't matter to me." He waited a long time and said, "Okay," and the door slammed and all the kids cracked up.

The little bus drove away. Some of the kids left and some sat down on the side of the road and watched the bus. I could hear the bus driver moving around. His seat squeaked until he stopped moving. Then it was really quiet. We just sat there together.

Soon it started to get a little bit dark out. I turned and looked right at him. He looked at me. It was the first time I ever saw him smile.

# Ellen Yeomans

WHAT REALLY HAPPENED

# STANDING UP ON THE BUS

Halfway through my third-grade year we got a new bus driver. Our old bus driver, Mike, was reassigned to the high school routes, and instead we got—well, I'll call her Belinda. I liked our old driver and I assumed I'd like Belinda, too. But while Mike was relaxed and friendly, Belinda was anxious and snappish. As the months went by, she became downright mean.

According to Belinda, we lived in a "horrible neighborhood." She mocked our parents and called us names. She began by calling us "animals." I had no idea that grown-ups could be so mean to kids. This was my first experience of someone not liking me without actually knowing me. The more Belinda tormented us, the more the kids on our bus acted up, until every day was nerve-racking. Students on her other runs, the kids who lived in "better" neighborhoods, never knew her to be cruel. I was a quiet, shy girl—at least on the bus, and at school—and I felt this injustice to my core.

As the months passed, Belinda added more names and more insults. And she became more creative with the way she made fun of our parents, our small houses, and the "trashy" neighborhood she had to drive in to pick us up and take us home. I hated the bus ride. By the time we got to school each day I had a stomachache. Daily, I wished Belinda would get transferred, or we would move, or I'd be allowed to quit school. Of course, none of that happened, and a couple of years with Belinda went by.

This was a small town with a small school district. Just about everyone knew everyone. My brothers and I complained to our parents about how Belinda treated us. At first, we protected our parents from that other truth: that she made fun of them and all the parents in our neighborhood. Later, we would share this, too. But I don't think our parents ever believed us. My mother dismissed our complaints, saying Belinda was a "good person," just a "nervous sort" and "overly sensitive." Our mom insisted we behave on the bus and not cause trouble.

One winter day, I'd had enough. I couldn't bear being called any more names or hearing again about our "good-for-nothing" parents. Just before my stop, on that full and rowdy bus, I put aside my fear of being noticed and stood up in the aisle. I shouted at Belinda that she was cruel. I told her she was an adult and should have better manners. The bus went absolutely silent. And then, I heard some kids behind me whispering that now I would be in big trouble. I was shaking, and I'm sure my face was red. I could feel it burning. Would I be kicked off the school bus forever? How would my parents drive me to school? Driving me would be impossible with their work schedules. And just how angry would my parents be when they found out what I'd done? What would be my punishment?

But Belinda said nothing as my brothers and I got off the bus. I was never called in to see the principal. My parents never knew. Things got a little better for a little while. Belinda continued to drive our bus, and the less she insulted us the more the kids behaved. But eventually, the shock of my outburst must have worn off because she went back to mocking us. However, it was never as bad as it had been before. It's possible Belinda uttered the worst insults under her breath or decided we weren't worth the energy to torment. A few years later my brothers and I moved on to middle school, and my younger sister never endured the same terrible treatment from Belinda.

I know now that she was a *bully*. Back then, I thought only other kids could be bullies, not adults. Driving a loud school bus in all kinds of weather must have been a misery for her. She certainly made it a misery for us. I try to see what would make someone act this way toward children. It seems she channeled all of her anxiety into picking on the people she valued the least: the kids who lived in the run-down neighborhood, the ones she figured were powerless to change things.

If I could, I would tell ten-year-old me to talk to my parents again. And if my parents wouldn't listen, I'd tell younger me to find *another* adult and tell *them*—again and again and again, until someone paid attention.

But first, I would congratulate the shy ten-year-old me who recognized how wrong our cruel bus driver was. That ten-year-old girl was brave. She stood up against a bully, took action, and shouted at injustice.

# Ellen Yeomans

## THE STORY

# SHE CALLS US NAMES

**Every Day**

Get on

quick

Sit down

quick

Don't look around

Don't sit up front

Don't sit far back

Don't get noticed

Middle is safest

Middle is invisible

You hope.

Every day.

**False Advertising**

Bright yellow buses

looked so cheery

on picture book pages,

on television screens,
in the tiny toy section of
Fay's Drugstore.
You thought it would be
friendly.
You thought it would be
fun.
You imagined singing.
You thought you'd swap sandwiches
with a bus best friend.
You thought wrong.

## You Thought About Telling

The first year
was confusing.
At some point
even though you knew,
    you understood
the pattern was every day
    it would always be every day
you decided not to tell.
You protected your parents
from the truth,
wanted them to think
    Everything was okay
    Everything was fine
    Everything was just like

the books on the shelf.

Besides, they knew her.

And they liked her.


## But This Year Is Different

You pose for the

First Day picture.

Your brother, your baby brother,

beside you this time,

finally old enough for school.


Your brother loves cars

He's the Vehicle Connoisseur

Cars, and trucks and planes,

but especially buses.

His love-worn

mini-metal one

in his pocket, right now

making his hands smell like pennies.

He is a little scared about school.

He is a lot excited about the school bus.

So why didn't you warn him?


Mom takes one last picture with the bus doors open

   behind you

with your brother turning away, ready to go.

   *Take your little brother's hand*

*Help him climb those big steps*
*Be sure to sit with him*
*Keep him safe*
*Have a great day at school!*
But you had to get there first.

## The First Mistake

Nod quick to the Driver.
Your brother tries to sit
in the empty front seat
across from little Mattie.
You jerk him out and up
hustle him down the aisle
select the right seat
turn to him
his lashes laced with tears
because you've hurt his shoulder
and hurt his heart.

> *I'm sorry, I'm sorry, I'm sorry*
> You whisper-shush him.
> *We can't sit up there.*
> *But my friend Mattie gets to*, he sobs.

He wants to see out that wide bus window,
he wants to pretend to steer
and shift.
He hopes to honk
that great bus horn.

He wants to see how the lights work
flash yellow, flash red.
Of course he does,
he's the Vehicle Connoisseur.

## She Calls Us Names

Tells us
We're animals
We're trash
We're poor
Our parents should never have had us.
We're monsters.
Why does she have to put up with such scum?

She's never hit anyone
Touched anyone
So what if you did tell?
Would she get in trouble?
Even if she has never hurt one of us?
Because she hasn't ever hurt one of us.
Right?

## The Bus Driver Says NO

When you try to bring little Mattie
back to the center seats with you.
She has an assigned seat now.
Mattie always smells

a little like cat pee

and a lot like wood smoke.

And no one sits with her.

Why didn't you try

to save her that first day?


## What If?

What if you lived closer to school? What if

    Mattie did?

What if you could convince them to move?

You'd be a Walker, not a Rider

And your brother would be a Walker, not a Rider

And you could "air out" Mattie all the way to school.

And all your problems would drive away.


## Side Effects

Every day you arrive at school

with a sore throat

trying to talk loud enough and long enough

to drown out whatever he might hear.

You can do this all year if you have to.

You will protect him his whole life if you have to.


Except

What if one day you are sick?

And next year you'll change schools.

Your baby brother won't. Then what?

**Holiday**

The day she is absent

is like the day before Christmas break

like the day before summer break.

And even though you have to go to school,

everyone is light

and loud

and happy.

If it could be like this every day

you could rest your voice.


**There Comes a Day**

Your voice is tired.

You are tired

of pretending that the ride is fine,

and you try to tell your parents

try to explain

and they love you

but they just don't see

what you see

can't hear

what you hear.

They ask your brother what he thinks

    *Sometimes Mattie gets picked on and*

    *some days the boys are rowdy*, he says.

He looks at you and you can see

that he is protecting too,

that he is protecting you.

Your parents say they're sorry

and they're sure it'll get better and soon.

And then they are laughing about when they were
	young

and the school bus hijinks they remember.

   But your brother's hands don't ever smell like

   pennies anymore.


## True

You ask Abby, who used to sit with you

before your baby brother went to school

You ask Abby,

   *Have you ever told? Do you think anyone ever has?*

Abby says, *My grandma told me to have more respect.*

   *My grandma says not to bother her and just*

   *behave.*

Keisha, beside her, leans forward and says,

   *I heard the Milton boys told last year. Principal said*

   *they misbehave on the bus. It'll be on their school*

   *record.*

Abby says, *It's true, they do.*

   *Some of us cut up when she calls us names*

   *and it's true*

   *everybody's a little poor over here.*

   *If we acted better, maybe she'd be nicer?*

**Try Again with Just Mom**

The bus kids must be exaggerating

because she is in the PTA

and helps out with the Cub Scout den.

Her own kids are good kids.

They'll talk to her at the next meeting

try to see what they can do to help get

the kids on the bus to behave.


**Now What?**

We've had a Stranger Danger Assembly

and a Bully-Free Zone Program

and two years of School Safety

and something like: Character-Counts-So-We-Won't-

    Tolerate-Bullies Day.

But none of that seems to fit what's happening here.


**That Day**

That Day Mattie

got yelled at because someone TOLD.

That Day Mattie got yelled at

because of the trash in piles by her front door

and her mother's dogs

that roam in the yards and stand in the street.

That Day Mattie got yelled at because she reeked

That Day Mattie cried and peed in the aisle

That Day you stood up and shouted,
*Leave Mattie alone!*
and the whole bus went dead quiet.
You took her to the too-busy school nurse
for some clean pants.
And the too-busy school nurse
looked at you funny when you said who made Mattie
cry.

## On the Bus

She told you to shut up so you do because you don't
want your brother to be her next target.
She told you to shut up so you do because you don't
want to be her next target.
She told you to shut up so you do because Mattie has
missed school since that day.
She told you to shut up so you do.
But you start writing everything down.

## This Time

you don't try to talk so much
that your brother won't hear.
Instead,
you write
every mean thing she says
with dates.
And then you borrow

what you aren't allowed to borrow

you borrow your mother's phone.

You will be in Big Trouble.

But you record it all

over and over

the curses

the comments

the names.

The way she taunts

Malcolm and Ginnie,

her new targets,

every time she stops at their house.

Tells them every time it looks like a pigsty.

Tells them every time how it suits them.

You feel your face redden

and try to nod and smile at Ginnie

so she knows you're on her side.

Of course, she does what you do,

doesn't look anyone in the eye

as she takes a seat.

If you don't look

you don't cry.

Usually.

### And Then

It happened pretty fast.

The too-busy school nurse

stopped and read

stopped and listened

to the video

on Mom's phone that you sneaked.

The not-too-busy school nurse called the principal

to see

to listen.

And they would have called Mattie

from her class if she had been to school since

the bus driver bullied her for the last time.

## New Driver

You let your brother sit up front

so he can pretend to drive.

Mattie sits in the seat across the aisle.

Not smiling

yet. But not crying

either.

Your brother calls over to Mattie,

uses his penny-scented hands,

shows her how to steer.

Mattie puts both hands on her pretend giant wheel

and steers like she knows exactly where to go.

Mike Winchell

# SCHOOL'S OUT

## Summer is here. You've made it!

After a long school year, it's time to kick back, relax, and soak up some rays. But . . . maybe your summer plans are different from what your parents have in mind. If that's the case, who knows what this summer might look like?

Author Holly Goldberg Sloan once had a summer of unexpected plans when she was a kid, and she couldn't help but write a story based on that unforgettable summer break.

# Holly Goldberg Sloan

## WHAT REALLY HAPPENED

# SOMEWHERE OVER THE RAINBOW

The newspaper in our town in Oregon came late every afternoon, so that at the end of the day my parents could always be found in the living room reading. Dinner table conversation sprang most often from an article they had just seen. My father was a professor of psychology at the local university. My mother had returned to school to get an architecture degree. But my mother loved movies and the theater.

I was in fifth grade and the shortest girl in my class. I was not musical, nor did I consider myself dramatic in any form. I liked drawing. My friends. Reading. Dogs. Bowling. And baking cookies. But on this night in late May so many years ago, as we sat down over chicken and salad and noodles with butter, my mother revealed that she had just read in the newspaper that the drama department at the university was holding auditions for parts in their summer stock play. They were looking for children (short was good) to fill the roles of the Munchkins in *The Wizard of Oz*. Seeing as we kids had no plans for the summer, did we want to audition? My older brother most certainly did *not*. My younger brother was usually up for something if I wanted to be involved. But I don't remember wanting to be involved. I remember clearly that my mother started singing "Over the Rainbow."

Two days later we were picked up at the curb in front of school and driven to the college campus. With Mom at our side, we signed in on a big sheet of paper and then made our way to a dark theater, where we waited until we were called, one by one, up onto the stage. A man sat at a piano, and each of us was asked to loudly announce our name and then take a turn singing. I believe we all tried to sing "Follow the Yellow Brick Road." But this might not be accurate. Memory has a way of bending things. It is very possible we were told we could sing anything we wanted for this audition. If that's the case, I feel fairly confident that I would have sung "This Land Is Your Land." I have no idea what my little brother picked.

However, this is what I do recall without question: The room was very dark when I was on that stage, and the light next to the piano was very bright. I did not believe then and I do not believe now (so many years later) that I have a good singing voice. What I have (then and now) is the confidence to do something without a lot of preparation or ability. I remember once the singing was over feeling nothing but relief to be back in the blue Buick station wagon and on the road. We were driven straightaway to the L & L Bakery, where my brother and I each got a chocolate cupcake with chocolate frosting for our efforts. This was a rare and impressive reward. It made the terror of the dark theater fade. Sort of.

That night when my mother put me to bed, I told her that I hoped my little brother would get the phone call (coming in four days only to the kids who were picked) to play the part of a Munchkin in the summer play. My mother smiled in a way that was thrilling and said I should know that my little brother told her only moments before that he wanted *me* to get the part. She was so proud of us. We were each hoping for the other to win. I'm not certain that I saw it as winning, although we were a competitive group. By the end of the four days the phone did ring, and there were two Munchkins in the house that summer. And the lessons I learned, as a kid working in the largest production of the year for the university's theater department, would stay with me for a lifetime.

*"Standing Tall" by Holly Goldberg Sloan is the basis for the novel* Short, *which will be published in January 2017 by Dial Books for Young Readers, an imprint of Penguin Random House.*

# Holly Goldberg Sloan

# STANDING TALL

'm small for my age, and most people think I look at least two years younger than a fifth-grader. But I'm used to people believing my younger brother and I are the same age.

School's out and I'm getting ready to do a lot of nothing, which is pretty much what every day is like in the summer. I have a bike that my neighbor Janis gave me, and I can ride down the hill. That's fun, but it means I have to push the bicycle back up the steep incline to get home. There are no gears on the pink hunk of metal, and being stuck with a heavy Schwinn with a rusty basket and rattling fenders can be a lot of work. The summer is for relaxing, so my plan is to leave it in the garage.

I don't mind walking most places. I cut through people's yards and make my way down to the flat streets to see my friends. It's almost as fast as riding the bike, because the road loops around the hill like the tail of a cat. My friends like to go bowling when we can get the money together. Once a week we take the bus downtown to the public library to check out books. The last few days we've been meeting up at the park on

Fairmont and practicing cartwheels. We're too old now to make up games on the swings, even though I still like to do that.

After the park we usually go to the drugstore to buy ice cream or candy. Last summer we bought a little turtle instead of chocolate. They were for sale in a big bowl of water at the checkout stand and were the size of Oreo cookies. They had dark green shells and a red stripe on their faces. We were going to share the tiny, swimming turtle—four of us girls would split her, and that would mean one week a month at each of our houses. But no one's parents went for the idea, and we had to return Petula. The store wouldn't give us our money back, which wasn't fair. We like to say we miss her, but that isn't true, because we only had her for two hours. According to Katie's mom, who is a doctor, we had put ourselves at risk for getting salmonella.

So far this summer everything's been going along according to plan, which is not to have a plan, and then yesterday my mom says that I should go audition at the university to be in some kind of play. She talks me into doing this before I can think it through. The next thing I know, I'm waiting with my little brother in a long line of kids. We have to sing on a stage in a very dark theater on campus. My dad teaches here, but not performing arts, which is what the building sign out front said. I listen to the adults talking as I wait my turn to sing and I hear a combination of voices.

"Six of the actors are *professionals*."

"Really?"

"That's what the woman in the office said. They're getting paid. One is flying out from New York."

"Anyone we would have heard of?"

"I guess we'll find out when they make their big announcement."

"The director's from Florida. He should be here. He's supposed to have worked on *Broadway*."

I'm happy that my mom isn't talking to these women. She's reading a book as we stand in line. My little brother, Randy, has a marble in his mouth. My mom doesn't know. He's way too old to have a piece of glass in his mouth, but he likes to do stuff like that, and I'm not going to rat him out, because maybe he's nervous standing here waiting to sing. I know I am. I hope Randy takes the marble out of his mouth when it's his turn, because he could choke to death.

Randy has a nice voice, and all year long he can be heard singing Christmas songs. He doesn't care that it's June. He still vocalizes about snow and sleigh bells and sounds good doing it. I'm not musical. Two years ago my parents bought a piano from some people who lived across town who were moving to Utah. Mom and Dad gave it to my two brothers and me for Christmas. I had to act really happy, because it was such a big present, but I pretty much hated the thing from the second it was carried into the basement, right next to my bedroom. The piano glared at me. It was like a dog that was chained up. It wanted to be set free and be played. But I just didn't have the talent.

Once a week, for almost two years, I had to go to this old lady's house right after school and take my lesson. The torture lasted for forty-five minutes. I learned the scales, because a person can probably do that in one class, but I didn't advance. Mrs. Sookram had other students and they were girls around my age, but I was lucky because we went to different schools. I never wanted the girl after me to hear me. She would know for sure how bad I was and that I was not progressing.

Part of the reason I wasn't progressing was because of the practicing. My fingers just didn't feel right on the keys. They didn't glide or find a mind of their own, which was what was supposed to happen. It was such a struggle, not like my big brother Tim and his music. He's thirteen years old and plays the guitar and he begs for his lessons. He practices for hours and hours in his room. Tim's guitar picks can be found all over the house. They're like the droppings of some kind of animal. Kids are just different, but he's firstborn, so he gave my parents unreasonable expectations.

But I did learn something in the two years of piano class with Mrs. Sookram. I learned how to make conversation with an adult and get them off track. I watch interview shows on TV, and the key to the whole thing is to ask a big first question, and then follow that with smaller ones that prove you are listening. My big question was always about Mrs. Sookram as a child. Where did she grow up and when did she know that she liked music?

If I got her going, which wasn't hard, she just floated back to a town in Idaho. I unraveled her past, piece by piece, week by week. I know more about this lady than about my own parents. She grew up on a potato farm, and she loved music so much that she walked every day to listen to a lady play a harp five miles away in the lobby of a hotel. I think the harp must be the saddest instrument to fall in love with because you can't haul it around with you, and also because it's not like a piano. You can't just go into someone's house and expect the person to point over to the corner and say, "Yeah, we've got a harp. Why don't you play us a song or something?"

Once I figured out that the old lady liked talking better than listening to me hit the wrong keys, the lessons were more manageable. But then one day she said, "Natalie, I'm going to call your mom this afternoon. I just don't feel right taking her money."

I wasn't sure what to say, but I managed, "She doesn't mind."

Mrs. Sookram looked like she was going to smile, but she didn't. She said, "Honey, I just don't think the piano is your instrument."

I nodded in a way that was half yes and half no. This involved sort of swinging my head around, and then I heard, "I'm going to miss you, Natalie."

She took my hand. It was way warmer than mine. I realized she was telling the truth because her eyes got all watery and stuff leaked out of her nose, and then I could see she was crying.

I should have said that I was going to miss her.

I wanted to say it, but a lie that big would have been impossible. So I put my arms around her waist and I gripped her really tight. She was a big lady, so there was a lot to hang on to. I felt lighter than air walking out the door and down her driveway. I didn't realize until I was on the sidewalk how much I hated the piano, and how much I'd learned about potato farming.

I pretty much haven't thought about music since, and now here I am waiting to sing "Over the Rainbow" with a zillion other kids at some big-deal audition that half the town has shown up for. I thought long and hard all day about what to wear to this torture session, and I settled on my leather sandals and my jean shorts and a white shirt that's called a peasant blouse. The shirt is my favorite, and it has puffy sleeves and a round neck and it's made of thin cotton. I didn't give the shirt the name "peasant blouse," because that's like saying "poor-person shirt." But that's just what they call these things. We don't have peasants in our area. We have some farmers just outside of town, and to my knowledge they hire workers, and don't have peasants in festive blouses pulling weeds. But what do I know?

Anyway, I have on what I consider to be one of my best outfits, and that's important, because one of the things I've learned is that it's good to feel comfortable with what you're wearing when you're going into a situation that is uncomfortable. There's only so much discomfort a person can take. My little brother has on a striped shirt and brown shorts with an elastic waist that I consider very unfashionable. And he has a marble in his mouth. We all make our own choices, except of course when it comes to the big things. Those decisions seem to be made for us.

After what feels like forever, it's my turn to get up on stage and sing. Most of the kids that went before me sang "Over the Rainbow." But I watched a girl ask the man at the piano if she could sing "Amazing Grace," and they didn't have a problem with that. So when I get to the piano I say, "Can I sing

'This Land Is Your Land'?" The guy nods and then winks at me. This is a nice thing to do, because his wink makes me think he knows something I don't know—like what I'm doing singing in front of two hundred strangers.

As I sing "This Land Is Your Land," I look right out at the auditorium. I don't want to be here, but I've been short all my life, and I guess I decided somewhere along the way not to be the kid who was short but also invisible. So I sing loud, and I make sure my hands aren't all knotted up in fists. I watched some of the other kids who went on before me, and they looked like they were ready to throw a punch. After I finish my song I look back at the piano player and say, "Thank you." He winks at me again. I can't help it—I laugh.

I guess my mom knows that today was hard on us, because we go right to the bakery and we each get a chocolate cupcake. We eat them in the car on the way home, even though dinner is only a half hour away.

I don't think about the audition until four days later. We had a water fight today at Katie's with big soaker shooters, and it went on forever and washed off some of my sunscreen, because I can feel my face tingle red. My mom is in the kitchen and she doesn't say anything, but she is really smiling when I come in. Instead my little brother yells, "Natalie, we're Munchkins!"

For a second I think he's saying I'm short, which of course I already know, but then my mom adds, "We got the call. You were *both* chosen!" I go through a lot of emotions. Mom and Randy are both smiling, and it seems as if we've won. But then

I start to think about this. *What about my summer? What about doing nothing? What about my friends and the park?* I still haven't mastered a good cartwheel.

I work on my plan for hours, but the next day when I try to explain that I sprained my ankle and can't go to the first rehearsal, my mom won't even listen.

There are other kids being dropped off as my brother and I walk into the theater. Most of the other kids have parents with them. Mom figured we could handle it, and she took off as soon as we were out of the car. I'm grateful for that now, especially when right away a woman with a clipboard tells the parents they can't stay and watch. We will be having "closed rehearsals."

The parents look really sad about this. I have no idea why they'd want to watch us turn into Munchkins (which we are told is going to take four full weeks). The woman with the clipboard tells them to go around to the front of the building and buy tickets now. We have eighteen performances, and she seems certain they will want to come every night and bring lots of friends. All I can think of is that four weeks of rehearsals and three weeks of performances is almost the whole summer. *Poof.* Gone.

Once they get rid of the parents, we are taken through the lobby into the theater. It is pretty dark in here, but I'm shocked to see three kids already up on the stage by the piano and two of the three are smoking! I can't believe this is happening. Who lets a ten-year-old smoke a cigarette? No wonder the parents were told to leave. I just can't wait to tell my mom and dad. My mom really doesn't like smoking, and this is going to change everything.

But then one of the three kids turns, and I see his face. That's when I realize he isn't a kid at all, because he has a beard! So he's a little adult. He's the perfect Munchkin. The rest of us are just big fakers, because as we get closer, I can see that these three have the right look. They are just like in the movie. It seems obvious to me now that there are not enough of these small people in our community to play Munchkins, so we kids are going to fill in.

I'm standing with my brother waiting with the group of kids, when the small woman comes over and sticks out her hand and says, "I'm Olive. Nice to meet you."

She goes to each kid and says the same thing, which breaks the ice. This causes the two men to come alive. The man with glasses is named Larry. The man with the beard is named Cookie. I don't think of Cookie as a man's name. It seems like something I'd name a small dog. Cookie is a lot older than Olive and Larry, and it doesn't take long before he explains he's been a performer all his life. He's mostly worked in circuses, but he's also had jobs as a clown in rodeos to distract the bucking broncos. Everything Cookie says is interesting. He's trained elephants, and he also can ride a unicycle and do a great backflip. After Cookie does a few tumbling moves, Larry warms up a bit. He knows how to talk in a funny voice and speak with crazy accents, plus he can make great animal noises.

The stage is a beehive of activity when Don, our director, shows up ten minutes later. Don is tall and thin, and he's dressed in what's called a jumpsuit, which means the top is connected to the bottom, sort of like the kind of coveralls a car mechanic wears. But Don's jumpsuit isn't navy blue. It's the color of a cantaloupe, and it has a fake belt that clips together in front with a gold buckle. Don's not wearing a costume. This is just his outfit, and I know this because I can see his wallet in his back pocket and it has a worn spot, which means the jumpsuit gets a lot of use. I try to think of my father wearing Don's orange outfit, and it just makes me go crazy inside. But somehow Don doesn't look strange in this piece of clothing, because he seems very comfortable with what he has on.

Don claps his hands together and shouts, "Performers! I need quiet!"

All of us stop making noise; even Cookie, who seems to love talking. Don then explains that we will work very, very hard. We will learn to sing and dance. We will be a team that works together with the main cast toward one goal: putting on a great show. He ends his big speech by saying, "I need the best from you. I need your brightest light! You will all shine! You are all my stars!"

I look over, and Olive is sort of crying. But she doesn't look sad, so maybe she's crying because she's so happy. Larry puts his arm around her, and then Cookie takes her hand. Across the stage a mirror is leaning against the back wall, and I glance in that direction and can see myself. I also spot my little brother, and I realize that somehow, without me even noticing, he's now taller than I am. But for the first time it doesn't matter. That's when I decide that this is going to be the summer that the short people call the shots. And moments later we are all singing "Follow the Yellow Brick Road."

# Mike Winchell

# SCHOOL ABROAD

**Just when you thought you'd** experienced everything school had to offer, suddenly a curveball gets thrown your way. You're going to school next year, all right—but you'll be taking classes in a whole new country.

Author Tommy Greenwald had this curveball pitched at him when he was young, so he took a swing at writing a story based on that year inside a foreign classroom.

WHAT REALLY HAPPENED

# HOW TO MAKE FRIENDS IN A FOREIGN COUNTRY

M y mom was way ahead of her time. Nothing she did surprised us: not that she'd kept her maiden name, not when she went back to college and then graduate school, not when she became a professor at a college three states away and lived there from Monday until Thursday every week.

Nope, nothing shocked us, until she came home one day and announced that she'd gotten a visiting professorship in Germany for a year, and she was taking my brother and me with her. I was in sixth grade; he was in seventh. We were smack in the heart of middle-school life—friends, sports, the occasional flirtation—in short, it was not the best time in the world to go live in a foreign country.

But it wasn't like we had a choice, so off we went. We ended up living in a small suburb of Bonn, which was then the capital of West Germany. There was a significant American military presence there, so my mother enrolled my brother and me in the local American school.

When I walked into my sixth-grade classroom, I noticed one thing right away: All the boys had crew cuts. It turned out everyone in the class was from a military family and had been living there for a number of years. And all the other students knew one another really, really well.

Let's just say I was a bit of an outsider.

This was new for me. Back home, I was a pretty social kid—not record-settingly popular or anything, but I had plenty of friends. But Germany was a very different story. For the first few weeks I was there, I sat alone at lunch, or occasionally with another kid or two who felt sorry for me. I had no buddies coming over after school. I had no girls passing notes to me when the teacher wasn't looking. Nobody even called me "Tommy"—they just called me "you" or "kid."

Then, one day, everything changed.

It had been a rainy morning. We got to school, took off all our rain gear, and stashed it in the hall. Our teacher, Mr. Williams—who wasn't very nice, by the way—launched into that day's lesson. Slightly bored, I glanced down, and noticed that I'd forgotten to put away my umbrella. It was dripping all over the floor.

*Oh, great,* I recall thinking.

I considered my options.

Should I raise my hand and tell Mr. Williams?

Absolutely not.

Should I just get up and take my umbrella out to the hall, dripping all the way, with everyone staring at me?

Forget it.

Should I close my eyes and magically transport myself back to peaceful, friendly Connecticut?

Yeah, good luck with that.

I decided to go with my fourth option: Stuff the thing out of sight without anyone noticing.

I bent down and tried to kick the umbrella farther under the desk, but things went wrong right away. First, it got stuck under my chair. Then, one of the spokes in the umbrella got bent. And finally, the kid next to me saw me and whispered, "What's going on?"

"Nothing," I whispered back. But that wasn't true. A lot was going on. And what was going on right then was me trying to figure out how to avoid a disaster.

The good news was: I managed to yank the umbrella out from under the chair.

The bad news was: As soon as I got it out, the umbrella opened with a big *pop!*

Actually, it was more like *POP!!!!*

Mr. Williams stopped talking. Every head in the room turned my way. I was sitting there with an open umbrella in my hand, in a classroom full of strangers, in a foreign country.

"May I ask what it is you think you're doing?" said Mr. Williams, in a scary "teacher" tone of voice.

Without thinking, I said the first thing that popped into my head:

"It looks like rain."

Mr. Williams cocked his head, like he couldn't quite believe what he had just heard.

I felt my face start to burn.

And then a couple of kids started to laugh. Then more kids. Until pretty soon, the whole class was laughing. At something I had said!

I felt my whole body relax, for what seemed like the first time in months.

Of course, I got in trouble. No recess for a week. But it was a small price to pay for the note that Jennifer Welbourne passed me in math later that day.

It said: *What's your name?*

# AMERICAN BOY

have wonderful news," said my mom, which meant one thing — she was about to tell me something completely *not* wonderful.

"What?"

She looked down at me as I lay in bed. "Well, you know how I told you that I might get transferred to England?"

"No," I said. My mom had a really important job, I knew that much. She wasn't home a lot. But England? I wasn't exactly sure where that was, but I was knew it was far away.

"Yes, you do, honey. We've talked about it several times."

"Well, maybe, but I don't want to go."

My mom sighed. "Well, I thought you'd be excited. Moving to Europe! Most kids would be thrilled at the opportunity. And besides, it's only going to be for a year or two."

Only? *Only?* I was in sixth grade — that's the big year, where everything matters. Where you make your friends that will last a lifetime. Where you figure out what you're interested in at school (if anything). And where you kiss your first girl, if you're superlucky and promise not to brag about it to everyone afterward.

"What about Dad?" I said. My parents were divorced, but that didn't mean my mom could just up and take me to another part of the world — did it?

"Your dad thinks it's a wonderful opportunity, and he's going to visit as often as he can," said my mom. Then she leaned over and kissed me. "I know it sounds hard, but this is going to be a wonderful adventure. Trust me."

After she turned out the lights, I lay in bed, trying to fall asleep.

*Trust me.*

When a parent says that, it's never a good sign.

★ ★ ★

Forty-three days later, I walked into a classroom in London, England, and about twenty heads turned in my direction.

The teacher, a man with long white hair who looked like he was about 106 years old, took off his glasses and looked me up and down. "Ah yes, the American boy," he said, in a way that made me think he wasn't all that crazy about American boys. "My name is Mr. Tiggle. Welcome to Year Seven, Room Four-A."

I was confused. "But I'm supposed to be in the sixth grade."

The twenty heads giggled.

"This is the equivalent of your sixth grade, son," said Mr. Tiggle. "Now please have a seat."

I sat down at the only empty desk, which was next to a brown-haired girl in pigtails.

"Hey, what's up?" I said.

The pigtailed girl looked at me like I had two heads, then turned away.

"Hey," whispered a boy with a crew cut. "You play football?"

*Okay*, I thought, *now we're getting somewhere.*

"I love football!" I exclaimed.

"Good," he said. "Meet us in the yard at lunchtime."

After two hours of trying to understand Mr. Tiggle's incredibly thick accent, it was time for lunch. Everyone streamed outside, the girls going one way, the boys going the other (at least some things were the same as in America). I looked for the boy from class but I couldn't find him, so I ended up sitting by myself on a bench in the corner, eating a sandwich.

"Hey."

I turned around. The kid from class was staring at me. Three of his friends were behind him.

"My name's Nigel," he said. "You said you play, right? Let's have a go." Then he kicked a soccer ball at me.

"This is a soccer ball," I told him. "I thought you said football."

Nigel snickered. "Riiiiight. A *soccer* ball." He said the word *soccer* as if it were a terrible disease. "Forget it then. Just give it back."

I picked up the ball and threw it to him.

"Oy, you stupid git!" said one of Nigel's friends. "You don't use your hands!"

Nigel shook his head. "Ah, what does he know, he's just an American boy," he said.

They all started laughing, chanting "American boy! American boy!"

And just like that, I had a nickname.

★ ★ ★

Three weeks later, I walked into the same classroom in London, England, and exactly one head turned in my direction.

"American boy," said Nigel, "would you mind not dripping all over my shoes?"

"Sorry," I murmured. It had been pouring rain all morning, and my windbreaker was soaked.

Nigel shook his head at me with a sneer. "You're supposed to put your rain gear in the hall."

"Right." I hurried back out just as Mr. Tiggle rushed by me and said, "Take your seat, please."

"Yes, sir."

I barely had time to take off my galoshes. As usual, I was the last one in my seat.

"Today we're going to be continuing our discussion of iambic pentameter," announced Mr. Tiggle. "Please open your books to page twenty-seven."

As I struggled to get my backpack open, I noticed that the girl with the pigtails—whose name was Anne—was staring in my direction.

I followed her eyes and looked down at myself. *Uh-oh.* Somehow, in the rush to get to my seat, I'd forgotten to take off my windbreaker. It was creating a pool of water that was starting to gather and run down the aisle—straight toward Mr. Tiggle.

"Uh-oh," I said, a little too loudly. A few kids glanced up. Nigel turned around, saw what was going on, and laughed.

"What did I say about the rain gear, mate?"

"Eyes forward," pronounced Mr. Tiggle, who was not yet aware that a stream was headed his way.

As the rest of the class went back to their books, I quickly and quietly tried to pull my jacket off over my head and stash it under my desk, where it could drip in private. The only problem was, one of the sleeves got tangled. Before I knew it, the whole thing was stuck on my head, and I couldn't see a thing.

I silently cursed my mom for not getting me a zippered windbreaker like I asked for.

Suddenly I heard a voice—it was my pigtailed neighbor, Anne, saying the first words she'd ever spoken to me.

"What are you doing? He's coming."

I stopped pulling and listened. Sure enough, I could hear the footsteps of Mr. Tiggle making his way down the aisle.

*SQUISH! SQUISH!* The footsteps were a little wet.

I heard titters, and whispers of *American Boy* bouncing around the classroom.

Mr. Tiggle arrived at my desk right as I was giving the windbreaker one last yank.

The good news was, I finally got it off.

The bad news was, it went flying in a very unlucky direction.

I looked up at him. There I was, sitting in a strange class-room in a strange city, in a strange country, in a school full of strangers who thought *I* was strange . . . with my waterlogged windbreaker sitting on top of my teacher's head.

It would have been hilarious if it had been happening to anyone else.

"May I ask what it is you think you're doing?" Mr. Tiggle hissed, water running down his face.

"Sorry?" I asked.

*"You heard me!"*

That was the moment I decided, the heck with it — I had nothing to lose.

"You had a little food on your face," I said to Mr. Tiggle. "Breakfast, probably. Just helping you wash it off."

The room fell dead silent. Mr. Tiggle's eyes narrowed to little slits. He looked like he was trying to decide whether to whip me or flog me (though I think they might be the same thing). Five seconds felt like five hundred seconds.

Until a kid in the front of the room started snorting.

Then a kid in the back of the room began wheezing.

And then, the next thing I knew, a wave was rippling around the room.

It was the unmistakable sound of kids cracking up. And Nigel was howling loudest of all.

Ah, laughter. The greatest sound ever, to a twelve-year-old boy.

*"Silence!"* thundered Mr. Tiggle. He threw the jacket down

on my desk and headed back to the front of the room, sidestepping the water. For a brief, idiotic second I thought maybe I was going to get off scot-free.

But no.

"See me after school, young man," Mr. Tiggle hissed, his voice barely above a whisper. "We'll get this sorted out, you and I."

I sighed, then put the still-dripping windbreaker under my desk. After two more hours of pretending to study poetry and verse, it was lunchtime. The rain had stopped, so I headed out to my usual spot—the far bench in the far corner—and ate my sandwich, daydreaming of home.

Just as I was finishing my last bite, there was a tap on my shoulder.

I looked up.

Nigel was standing there, with a ball in his hand. Next to him were his friends Graham and Ian, and standing behind him was pigtailed Anne.

I braced myself for the usual round of teasing, but when I looked at Nigel's face, I could tell something was different. He was smiling, as usual, but his eyes were different. They weren't cold. They weren't distant. They weren't suspicious.

They were open.

"Hey, American Boy," he said. "Let's play soccer."

# Acknowledgments

## Mike Winchell

The same collection of people who were acknowledged in the first book played a major role in this book, especially my family, and I'd like to thank them again for their continued support. Specifically, my brothers, Jeff and Tim; my sister-in-law Corrine; my mother, Gerrie White; my stepfather, Garry White; my father, David; and, of course, my collection of cool nieces and nephews: Alex, Rhiannon, Luke, Madison, McKenna, Jillian, Vincent, Rhys, and Maya. On my wife's side: my mother-in-law, Lydia; my brothers-in-law, Mark, Phillip, and Jeff; and my sister-in-law Connie. My wife, Shelby, is my rock and always will be, and my kids, A.J. and Savannah, are our sole purpose in life. Yes, I have an amazing family. Thank you all for everything.

My agent, Brianne Johnson, is a butt-kicking champion for me and all her clients, and without her no book with my name on it would grace the shelves. My editor extraordinaire, Bonnie Bader, and her trusty sidekick, Renee Hooker, are the best. You two made everything run smoothly. Art director Sara Corbett was accidentally left out of my round of nods in the first book, but without her presence we wouldn't have the awesome artwork in this book. Speaking of artwork, I lucked out when Eglantine Ceulemans took on the task of designing our cover art for the first book, so a belated "thank you" to her, because I am in awe of her work. And I will continue to say that the entire Grosset & Dunlap team is amazing; I'm incredibly lucky to have found a true home for this project. Francesco Sedita is a visionary who knows how to compose an orchestra of publishing professionals, and I thank him for believing in this project.

Thanks to the many writing friends and publishing professionals who have helped me along the way: Tracy Edward Wymer, John Zeleznik, Shaun Hutchinson, Mollie Glick, Henry Neff, Rebecca Taylor, Paul Murphy, Amber Lough, Alison DeCamp, Gail Nall, Monica Tesler, David Kazzie, Evelyn Skye, Alan Lawrence Sitomer, Matthew J. Kirby, and Lisa Mangum.

I'd like to thank my "neighbors" Bruce Coville and Ellen Yeomans for not only being a part of this collection but for their selfless guidance and advice ever since I began my foray into publishing. Bruce and Ellen, we all know you're talented writers, but I would like to thank you even more for simply being great, genuine, high-character human beings.

Finally, the late Stuart Scott (1965–2015) was not a close friend of mine, and we corresponded through digital means only, but I want to thank him for his help when I needed it. His brief advice grounded me in the true meaning of life: being the best father you can be, every single day. In turn, I'd like to thank his daughters, Sydni and Taelor, for sharing their father with the world. Girls, your father was a class act. He's beaming with pride from up above.

# Authors

**SHAUN DAVID HUTCHINSON** is the author of *The Deathday Letter*, *fml*, *The Five Stages of Andrew Brawley*, *We Are the Ants*, and the forthcoming *Center of the Universe*, and the editor of the school shooting anthology *Violent Ends*. He lives with his partner and dog in South Florida and watches way too much TV. Visit him at www.shaundavidhutchinson.com.

**HOWARD CRUSE**'s comics and cartoon illustrations have appeared in numerous newsstand magazines and underground comic books. His column "Loose Cruse" was a regular feature in *Comics Scene* magazine; his comic strip *Wendel* ran in the *Advocate* during much of the 1980s; and he has enjoyed stints as a cartooning instructor at the School of Visual Arts in New York and at the Massachusetts College of Liberal Arts in Massachusetts, where he and his husband, Ed Sedarbaum, have been living since 2003.

Cruse has published nine books, the best-known being the internationally award-winning 1995 graphic novel *Stuck Rubber Baby*, translations of which have been published in Germany, France, Spain, Italy, and Poland. Visit him at www.howardcruse.com.

**MEG MEDINA** writes picture books and middle-grade and young-adult fiction that examines how cultures intersect, as seen through the eyes of young people. Her young adult novel *Yaqui Delgado Wants to Kick Your Ass*, earned the 2014 Pura Belpré Award among numerous other distinctions. Her most recent books are *Burn Baby Burn* (Candlewick Press, 2016) and *Mango, Abuela, and Me*, a Junior Library Guild selection.

In 2014, Meg was named one of the CNN 10 Visionary Women in America for her work to support girls, Latino youth, and diversity in children's literature. Visit her at www.megmedina.com.

**BRUCE COVILLE** has published more than one hundred books for children and young adults, including the international best seller *My Teacher Is an Alien* and the Unicorn Chronicles series. His works have appeared in a dozen languages and won children's choice awards in as many states. He has been a teacher, a toymaker, a magazine editor, a gravedigger, and a cookware salesman. He is also the founder of Full Cast Audio, an audiobook publishing company devoted to producing full-cast, unabridged recordings of material for family listening. Mr. Coville lives in Syracuse, New York, with his wife, illustrator and author Katherine Coville. Visit him at www.brucecoville.com.

**WENDY MASS** is the *New York Times* best-selling author of *The Candymakers* and fifteen other novels for young readers. They include *A Mango-Shaped Space*, *Jeremy Fink and the Meaning of Life* (recently made into a movie), the Willow

Falls series that began with *11 Birthdays*, and *Every Soul a Star*. Just out is *Pi in the Sky* and a new series for beginning readers called Space Taxi. She is currently writing the sequel to *The Candymakers* while building a labyrinth in her backyard in New Jersey. Not at the same time, of course. That'd be weird. Visit her at wendymass.com.

**JACQUELINE WEST** is the author of the *New York Times* best-selling middle-grade series The Books of Elsewhere (Dial/Penguin) and the young adult novel *Dreamers Often Lie* (Dial/Penguin, April 2016). Her books have been selected by the Junior Library Guild, garnered many awards and nominations, and been published in eleven other countries to date. Her short fiction for young readers has appeared in *Spider*, the *School Magazine*, and the anthology *Starry-Eyed* (Running Press, 2013). She lives with her family in Red Wing, Minnesota, surrounded by large piles of books and small piles of dog hair. Visit her at www.jacquelinewest.com.

Raised by wolves just outside Los Angeles, **BRUCE HALE** has written and/or illustrated more than thirty-five books for kids. His popular series include the award-winning Chet Gecko Mysteries, School for S.P.I.E.S., and Clark the Shark.

When not writing or illustrating, Bruce loves to perform. He has appeared on stage, on television, and in an independent film called *The Ride*. A Fulbright Scholar in Storytelling and a member of the National Speakers Association, Bruce has spoken at schools, conferences, and libraries from New York to New Delhi.

These days, Bruce lives in Santa Barbara with his wife, his sweet mutt, Riley, and his massive collection of hats.

Visit him at www.brucehale.com.

**SARAH PRINEAS** is the author of the Magic Thief series, which has been published in twenty languages. In addition to being a 2009 E. B. White Read Aloud honor book and an NCTE Notable book, *The Magic Thief* appeared on sixteen state reading lists. Her latest books are *The Magic Thief: Home* and *Ash and Bramble*, her first young adult book. Sarah has a PhD in English literature and lives in the Iowa countryside with her mad scientist husband, two odd children, two perfectly normal cats, chickens, bees, a bunch of goats, and the best dogs in the world. Visit her at www.sarah-prineas.com.

**C. ALEXANDER LONDON** has written books for children, teens, and even a few grown-ups. He's the author of more than twenty books, including the Accidental Adventures series, the Dog Tags series, and the talking animal epic *The Wild Ones*, for middle-grade readers. His young adult debut, *Proxy*, was a 2014 Top Ten Quick Pick for Reluctant Young Readers and has been on several state reading lists. He lives in Brooklyn, New York, where he can be found wandering the streets talking to his dog, who is the real brains of the operation.

**NATE EVANS** has illustrated more than thirty-five kids' books and written a few more. The latest of these is a graphic novel for middle-grade readers titled *Tyrannosaurus Ralph*, with art by Vince Evans. Nate has also coauthored several picture books with Laura Numeroff, including *Ponyella* and the Jellybeans series. *Ponyella* and two of the Jellybeans books appeared on the *New York Times* Best Seller list. Visit www.nateevans.com.

**VINCE EVANS** has been belch battling for years. Showing great promise at an early age, he quickly won the junior title and went professional. Unable to gain weight and compete in the more lucrative heavyweight category, Vince was eventually forced to supplement his income fighting in Back Alley Burp Battles. It was during one of these bouts that he was injured by a Bouncing Betty Blast and forced to retire. He now lives in a home for aging belch boxers, where his brother, Nate, visits him every Tuesday night, bringing him warm, shredded cabbage and reading him kids' books. Vince is only interested in the pictures, but listens politely. Missing the excitement of belch boxing, Vince followed Nate into the dangerous world of children's books, where he writes and illustrates and still struggles to become a heavyweight.

**VARIAN JOHNSON** is the author of six novels, including *The Great Greene Heist*, an ALA Notable Children's Book Selection, a *Kirkus Reviews* Best Book of the Year, and a Texas Library Association Lone Reading Star List selection. Varian was born and raised in Florence, South Carolina, and attended the University of Oklahoma, where he received a BS in civil engineering. He later attended the Vermont College of Fine Arts, where he received an MFA in writing for children and young adults. Varian now lives outside of Austin, Texas, with his family. Visit him at www.varianjohnson.com.

**DON TATE** is an award-winning author and the illustrator of numerous critically acclaimed books for children. Books he's authored include *It Jes' Happened: When Bill Traylor Started To Draw* (Lee and Low Books), an Ezra Jack Keats New Writer Honor winner; and *Poet: The Remarkable Story of George Moses Horton* (Peachtree). He is the illustrator of *Whoosh! Lonnie Johnson's Super Stream of Ideas* (Charlesbridge); *The Amazing Age of John Roy Lynch* (Eerdmans); *Hope's Gift* (Putnam); and *Ron's Big Mission* (Dutton). Don is a founding host of *The Brown Bookshelf*—a blog dedicated to books for African American young readers—and a member of the #WeNeedDiverseBooks campaign, created to address the lack of diverse, nonmajority narratives in children's literature. He lives in Austin, Texas, with his family. Visit him at www.dontate.com.

**KELLY STARLING LYONS** is a children's book author whose mission is to transform moments, memories, and history into stories of discovery. Her books include the CCBC Choices-honored picture book *One Million Men and Me*; *Ellen's Broom*, a Junior Library Guild selection and Coretta Scott King Illustrator

Honor winner; and *Tea Cakes for Tosh* and *Hope's Gift*, Notable Social Studies Trade Books for Young People. Her title *One More Dino on the Floor* debuted in 2016 and *Jada Jones: Rock Star* debuts in 2017. Find out more at www.kellystarlinglyons.com.

A former textbook writer, **STEVE SHEINKIN** is now making amends by writing history books kids and teens actually *want* to read. Recent titles include *Bomb*, *The Port Chicago 50*, *The Notorious Benedict Arnold*, *Lincoln's Grave Robbers*, and the newest, *Most Dangerous*, a finalist for the 2015 National Book Award. His books have won numerous awards, including a Newbery Honor, the Siebert Medal, and the YALSA Award for Excellence in Nonfiction for Young Adults. Read more at stevesheinkin.com.

**ELLEN YEOMANS** is the ghostwriter of a middle-grade series published by Penguin. She is the author of a young adult novel, *Rubber Houses* (Little, Brown Books for Young Readers, 2007), as well as the picture book *Jubilee* (Eerdmans Books for Young Readers, 2004) and the upcoming picture book *The Other Ducks* (Neal Porter Books/Roaring Book Press, 2017). She is the New York State Regional Advisor Emeritus for the Society of Children's Book Writers and Illustrators. Ellen received her MFA in writing from Vermont College of Fine Arts and teaches a number of writing classes throughout central New York.

**HOLLY GOLDBERG SLOAN** is a *New York Times* best-selling

author, screenwriter, and film director. Among her books are *Counting by 7s*, *Appleblossom the Possum*, and *I'll Be There*. She has written a number of successful feature films, including *Angels in the Outfield* and *The Big Green*. Holly was born in Michigan and spent her childhood in Holland, Turkey, Washington DC, Berkeley, California, and Eugene, Oregon. She is a graduate of Wellesley College and the mother of two sons. Holly lives with her husband, Gary A. Rosen (the illustrator of *Appleblossom the Possum*), in Santa Monica, California. Her website is www.hollygoldbergsloan.com/.

**TOMMY GREENWALD** is the author of the Charlie Joe Jackson series and the Crimebiters! series for children, among other books. He is a cofounder of Spotco Advertising in New York and the lyricist of *John and Jen*, an off-Broadway musical. Tommy has also contributed humor pieces to the *New York Times*. For occasionally updated information, please visit tommygreenwald.com.